THE
Lost Gospel OF
DONALD

A satire by

DR. PRESTON COLEMAN

Satirica Press   Oxford, MD

Print ISBN: 978-1-09830-600-7
ebook ISBN: 978-1-09830-601-4

This is a work of fiction. All names, characters, places, and events are products of the author's imagination or used fictitiously. Resemblances to actual persons, living or dead, places, and events are purely coincidental.

Satirica Press
Box 373
Oxford, MD 21654
www.satiricapress.com
www.prestoncoleman.com

Printed in the United States of America

10 9 8 7 6 5 4 3 2 1

FOREWORD

In addition to the four gospels found in the authorized version of the Bible, dozens of alternative gospels have surfaced through the years. These "lost gospels" include the Book of Mormon, discovered by amateur magician Joseph Smith in Wayne County, New York, in 1823, and the so-called Gnostic Gospels, 52 manuscripts written by various authors and found by two farmers digging for fertilizer near Nag Hammadi, Egypt, in 1945.

Some of these gospels were purportedly written during or shortly after the life of Jesus by authors who knew him, including the apostles Thomas, Andrew, Philip, and Bartholomew, as well as a gospel attributed to "Mary," whom some believe to be Mary Magdalene, and others, the mother of Jesus. Perhaps the most controversial of these lost gospels is attributed to Judas Iscariot, the supposed betrayer of Jesus, in which he claims to have been following Jesus's instructions with the infamous kiss in the Garden of Gethsemane that identified our Lord to the authorities.

The most recently discovered gospel was found by a plumber in the basement of a Russian Orthodox church in Weehawken, New Jersey, in 2019.

Little is known about its author, Donald of Gaul. Analysis of the text suggests that he was the son of a Germanic warlord from Avaricum, a center of barbarian culture and the spot where Julius Caesar first encountered Vercingetorix in the Great Gallic Revolt of 52 BC. Donald appears to have been born a few years before Jesus into a prominent family whose wealth allowed him to immigrate to Rome, where he built a series of inns, taverns, bath houses, casinos, and theatres, first in the Roman capital, and later throughout the Mediterranean region.

According to his gospel, Donald was present when John the Baptist baptized Jesus at Bethabara, where he took an immediate interest in the prophet and the aspiring messiah, whom he aggressively recruited to work as magicians in his hospitality empire. He also claims to have been present at the Transfiguration, Crucifixion, Resurrection, and Ascension and to have catered the Last Supper.

His substantial wealth and real estate holdings distinguish Donald from other gospel authors, most of whom were from the lower and middle classes. His experience in business and entertainment deeply informs his writing, further distinguishing his from the more spiritual perspectives of other gospel authors, as does the extensive use of the first person.

One last difference should be noted. While the other gospels were found on various media including sheets of parchment, papyrus scrolls, clay tablets, and in the case of the Book of Mormon, golden plates, the gospel of Donald was written in brief snippets of one to three hundred characters on small tissues of papyrus and scraps of cloth.

Archaeologists speculate that these tissues and scraps may have been used in Donald's businesses to record notes. He apparently traveled with a contingent of secretaries who performed a variety of tasks for him, including recording his conversations with Jesus and others and compiling his own voluminous scribblings. According to excavators working with the Herculaneum Conservation Project in the sewers of Herculaneum and Pompeii, similar tissues and scraps may also have been used in the ancient world as toilet paper.

Whatever their origin, these notes have now been meticulously re-assembled and translated into English from the original Vulgar Latin by linguists at the Gnostic Institution, Inc., in beautiful downtown Burbank, California. The resulting text is published here for the first time. To make the gospel more accessible to modern readers, the vernacular used in the original has been updated as appropriate.

THE GOSPEL ACCORDING TO DONALD OF GAUL

1 In the beginning was the Word. I have the best words, my words are the best. No one has better words than me, they're fantastic.

2 Now a lot of people have told the story of this guy, Jesus. I've heard these stories, they're okay, some of them are okay, some of them, frankly, aren't so great.

3 And don't believe what the fake scribes say, not about Jesus, and not about me. These fake scribes, they're totally fake, phony, the enemies of the people. Very dishonest, these scribes, totally dishonest.

4 So this Jesus, he was a pretty good guy, okay? I'm here to tell you he was a pretty good guy. And he had a terrific career, he put on one helluva show. But he could've been so much more if he'd just listened to me. I could've made him a star, the biggest star, a real A-lister.

5 I was there when he was just becoming famous. He came out of nowhere, then bing! bang! bong! He was known all over the Roman Empire. He really knew how to make a scene, I can tell you that. It happened like this, you should have been there:

6 Before Jesus, there was this Jew, he called himself John the Baptist. He was famous, very famous, in the eastern Mediterranean, where I was expanding my hospitality business. He worked over in Judea, around the Jordan River. He was in the traveling preacher racket.

7 People came from all over Judea and Samaria and Perea to see him preach, because they thought he wasn't just another preacher, but, like, some kind of prophet or something. Holy cow, a prophet! Now that's branding, and I know branding, it's what I do best.

8 But that wasn't all. This Jew, John the Baptist, he didn't just stand there and preach, like most people in that racket. He had a gimmick. You have to have a gimmick, that's show business. See, he dunked people in the river—bent them over backwards and shoved them right under the water, to clean off their sins, if you can believe that.

9 The Jews over there loved him, they ate this stuff up. He even had Herod Antipas, the King of the Jews, worried, he riled the people up so bad. And if the King of the Jews was worried, the emperor was worried. (That was Tiberius Caesar, the Emperor of Rome. I'll get to those guys later, though.)

10 So, cleaning off sins, you're probably wondering what that's all about. I know I did. These Jews, they're funny people, they're full of guilt, everybody knows that. So he gets rid of their guilt, just washes it away. That's what he's selling. A marketing genius, I'm telling you. Figure out what the people want, and give it to them.

11 Well, if people were buying it, I didn't care *why* they were buying it, I just wanted to sell it. I figured, maybe we could take this guy on the road performing at my properties. He would've been a natural to perform in my bathhouses, it would have been pure gold. Or I could've set him up at the brand new Donald Inn in Jerusalem and made a bundle.

12 Besides, come on, dunking pretty girls in a river—who wouldn't want to see *that*? What a gimmick! My bath houses did great with the wet tunic contests. Gorgeous girls in tight white tunics getting drenched with cold water, just imagine! You should see it, it's fabulous.

13 And to be perfectly honest, that's what I thought was going on. Sure, some people would come to see a preacher, and more would come to see a prophet. But more, a lot more, would come to see girls in wet tunics, right? That gimmick was gold, it was spectacular.

14 At the Donald Bath by the Forum in Rome—that's my biggest bath complex, it has everything, baths, food, massages, dancing girls—we have the biggest wet tunic contests. They're amazing, they're practically pageants. We sell tickets by the thousands.

15 I'll go backstage, before a show, and everyone's getting dressed and ready and everything else. And I'm allowed to go in because I'm the owner, and therefore I'm inspecting it. You know, I'm inspecting, I want to make sure everything is good. They're standing there with no clothes, and you see these incredible looking women, and so I sort of get away with things like that.

16 I was planning on expanding into Judea anyway, so I took my yacht across the Mediterranean into the port of Caesarea Maritima, which was built by my friend, King Herod the Great. Great guy, Herod, he was Herod Antipas's father. Pretty good builder, too, but not as good as me.

17 Herod the Great renovated the Temple in Jerusalem, too, the one that was destroyed by the Babylonians. I'll give him credit, it was a great restoration. By the time he finished it, it was, like, really big, the biggest thing in that part of the empire.

18 Not bad, that temple. He expanded it into a top-notch mixed-use development, but he could have used a better architect if you ask me. I could have done it better, way better, that I can tell you.

19 But Herod, he didn't put his name on it, which was stupid, totally stupid. You should put your name on everything, build that brand, never stop building it, like my dad always used to say. That's what I do, and look at me, I'm rich, very rich. I'm worth billions and billions, believe me.

20 It's all about branding. The Great Pyramid of Cheops, The Tower of David, Caesar's Palace—you get the picture. You have to put your name out there every chance you get.

21 Boy, did I make an entrance in Caesarea! "Donald" in huge letters on every sail, dancing girls, drummers, jugglers, you name it. The whole town came out to see me. It was something, let me tell you. Like I said, *branding*!

22 Hundreds of people were there, maybe thousands. I heard five thousand. Who knows, maybe ten thousand, people were saying that. Always make an entrance, that's what I say, and make it big. A big entrance, that's what people like.

23 We spent the night at the best inn in town—it was a dump compared to my inns, but what can you do—then we took a caravan down to the Jordan River. I rode in a golden chariot behind an Arabian horse, a beautiful black one, the best I could find. "Donald" was written everywhere, on the chariot, on the banner, on the horse, everywhere.

24 We get to the Jordan at a town called Bethabara, not far from Jericho. Jericho, not much of a town in my opinion, a real shithole. They didn't build the best walls, I can tell you that. They should've let me build them a wall. I build the best walls, I would build a great wall, nobody builds walls better than me.

25 So anyway, there he was, John the Baptist, knee-deep in the river. You should have seen this guy, he was a mess, a real mess, a total disaster. He was a short little guy, a runt, and all he had on was a leather jock strap and a camel hide. It was pathetic, what a letdown. I couldn't believe I came all that way to see such a loser.

26 They said he lived off wild honey and locusts. Who the hell eats locusts? What kind of way is that to live? Fish eggs and snails, that I understand, but grasshoppers? And a leather jock strap and camel hide? Who dresses like that? This guy John, he was crazy, I mean, batshit crazy. So I call him John the Batshit, that's what I call him.

27 Anyway, there were hundreds of people there, maybe a thousand. I heard a thousand, but that wasn't as many as I had in Caesarea. Not even half of my crowd. I'm thinking maybe a tenth at the most. I get the biggest crowds, absolutely the biggest, you should see my rallies back in Rome.

28 There was a line of Jews, like, half a mile long waiting to get dunked in the water. I didn't see the point, to be perfectly honest. They thought he was washing away their sins, this John the Batshit, can you believe that? It was crazy, totally crazy.

29 He called it the "remission" of sins. A pretty fancy word, "remission." It means forgiveness, they tell me, but what the hell, who needs that? I sure don't need to be forgiven, that's for losers. I've never done anything to be forgiven for as far as I'm concerned. But these Jews and their guilt, good grief!

30 So he's dunking and preaching, preaching and dunking. Now don't get me wrong, he could preach up a storm, that John guy. And the dunking was nice, but you could see a better wet tunic contest at any bath house in the empire.

31 Then I hear some people asking if this John guy was their savior. These Jews, they were expecting their god, they call him Yahweh—I call him NoWay— to send them a savior or something. They call this savior the messiah, the Christ, and they're expecting him, like, anytime now.

32 Out of nowhere, this John, all of a sudden he throws up his hands and yells, "I indeed baptize you with water; but one mightier than I comes, the latchet of whose shoes I am not worthy to unloose; he shall baptize you with the Holy Ghost and with fire!" Then he goes right back to dunking and preaching, preaching and dunking.

33 Well that was weird, because these people, they wore sandals, not shoes. What the hell a Holy Ghost is, I don't know. I don't believe in ghosts. And who the hell wants to be baptized with fire? Like I said, I didn't get it.

34 And besides, who talks like that? He had a funny way of talking. It sounded like a script to me, like he was reading out of a book. I don't need a script, I just wing it. I know words, my words are the best. No scripts for me.

35 There were some beautiful women there, and some very pretty girls, too. There's nothing like a nice wet tunic to show off a fine figure, trust me on that. I had this secretary from Gomorrah with me, she was a ten, let me tell you, a real looker.

36 I wanted to see this secretary from Gomorrah—I always keep two or three secretaries around for this, that, and the other—I wanted to see this girl get dunked something awful, and I wasn't going to wait. Waiting is for losers.

37 So we busted in line. I had to shove some joker out of the way, grabbed him by the arm and bam! Off he went. He was a hillbilly from over by Macedonia, some place called Mount Black they tell me. Just another loser as far as I'm concerned, this guy, but who cares. Some people whined about it, but they got over it.

38 We wind up in the front of the line, right behind a bunch of sisters, every one of them a nine or a ten—do I know how to cut in line, or what—and a scraggly little guy in a dirty white robe. Those sisters were a sight to behold. Any one of them could have danced at my baths in Rome and done just fine.

39 John gave them all a good dunking, but he kept the line moving. He should have lingered on the best-looking ones and let us guys get an eyeful, but he didn't. Not so bright, in my book, not so bright. You have to put on a show, it's all about the showmanship.

40 Well, after these sisters, there was this little guy in the dirty white robe, then my girl from Gomorrah was next in line, so I told him to hurry the hell up and get it over with. Good looking guy, a bit thin, but he had a nice face.

41 He didn't get mad, he just smiled at me kind of sad—he had the saddest smile, it was a little creepy if you ask me—and bowed his head a little, then he waded right on out to John the Batshit. And that's when the show really began.

42 Now, these two must have had their schtick all planned out, because John stopped cold when he saw this guy. He just froze for the longest time, looking him right in the eye, and everything got real quiet.

43 And then he said, "I have need to be baptized of you, and come you to me?" Yeah, he talked like that, John the Batshit did.

44 And this guy just gave that same sad smile and said—he had this funny way of talking, too—**Allow it to be so now: for thus it becomes us to fulfill all righteousness.**

45 Like I said, they must have had their schtick all planned out, because a few people in the crowd—they must have been shills, I know a shill when I see one—these shills started saying all kinds of things.

46 "That's him," says this one guy, pointing at John, "the one the prophet Isaiah said would come like a 'voice of one crying in the wilderness' to prepare the way for the Lord!" "Sure enough," says this other guy, "The prophet said, 'Prepare you the way of the Lord, make his paths straight.'"

47 That's how prophets talk, see. These Jews, they have more prophets than they know what to do with, and prophets don't talk like the rest of us.

48 John the Batshit, and the guy in the dirty white robe, and the shills—well, they were all talking funny and highfalutin. If that doesn't sound like people reading a script, I don't know what does. And I know scripts, I'm in show biz. My theaters are the best, I put on the best shows, they're terrific.

49 I figured out right away that it was all a put on, a setup. They were acting like John the Batshit was a prophet, and this guy in the dirty white robe was the Christ—this savior, this messiah, that the Jews were expecting.

50 That's crazy, of course, there's no such thing as a messiah. So the jig was up, at least as far as I was concerned. But I guess if you're going on the traveling preacher circuit, you might as well go all out.

51 And these guys, John and Jesus, they weren't just about the preaching, or even the dunking and the wet tunics. No sir, they were into magic and faith healing and miracle working, the whole nine yards. They were the best magicians I ever saw, they were fabulous.

52 Anyway, everyone was pretty freaked out, let me tell you. The crowd was buzzing. Then the show really began, and I mean, it was amazing. You're not going to believe it, but I was there, I saw it all.

53 I don't know how they did it, but at just the right moment, these sunbeams broke through the clouds. It was beautiful. And then this big white dove—magicians use doves all the time, everyone knows that—this dove came floating down and landed smack on the scraggly guy's shoulder.

54 That was Jesus, if you haven't figured it out already. But what a trick that was! How they did it, I have no idea, but it was big league, I mean, the biggest.

55 These shills, and there were plenty of them, started yelling, "Oh, it's the Holy Ghost!" "Look, it's the Holy Spirit!" "Holy Moses, it's the Spirit of God!" Pretty big talk for a dove, I thought. But the crowd bought it.

56 After that, there was a clap of thunder, and this huge voice, I mean, really huge, comes out of nowhere—supposedly the voice of God, you know, Yahweh, or NoWay. And it sort of clears its throat—ahem, ahem!—and pauses sort of dramatic-like.

57 And then it says, ***"This is my son, in whom I am well pleased."*** Well, that was a little over the top. I mean, who says "whom" anymore? It sounds so snooty. But I guess, if you're playing a god, you have to talk like a god. You have to stick with the script.

58 But what a ventriloquist! You should've heard him! He was the best ventriloquist I ever heard, and I've hired plenty of ventriloquists to work my properties, believe me.

59 What with the propheting, and the sunbeams, and the dove, and the thunder—well before you know it, they were calling this Jesus the son of a god. Actually, they were calling him *The Son of God!*

60 If you don't know, these Jews, they only believe in one god, this Yahweh. Seriously, just one? Great Jupiter, the Greeks have ten or twelve, I think, and the Romans and us Gauls have tons of them. They're all made up, anyway, so why stick with just one? Why not have a thousand, like the Hindoos?

61 Funny people, these Jews, but great negotiators, and great businessmen. Always trying to get a monopoly, the Jews. If you're going to have a monopoly, that's a pretty good monopoly to have—the one and only God. Am I right, or what?

62 Well, *I* wasn't fooled, I can tell you that. But the crowd went wild, they were eating it up. Everyone crashed the stage—in this case, the bank of the river, but I know a stage when I see one—and started screaming and trying to touch Jesus. John tried to hold them back, at least he pretended to, but that was all part of the show.

63 I didn't stick around, I'd seen enough. Whoever he was, this guy Jesus, he was a first-rate magician, the best I'd ever seen, and he had one helluva side-kick, this John the Batshit. One of them, I figured it was Jesus, was an incredible ventriloquist, too. He was the best ventriloquist, absolutely the best I ever saw. I saw him do that voice of god thing in his act a couple more times, but we'll get to that later.

64 So I'm in the hospitality business, see? Inns, taverns, casinos, bath houses, theaters—I've got them all. And what's the key to the hospitality business? Entertainment, that's what. I knew I could make a fortune if I could get these two to come to Rome and perform in my shows. Holy Bacchus, we could pack any arena, fill the Forum, sell out the Circus Maximus! Take it on the road and ride the gravy train, baby!

65 And who would be the Master of Ceremonies? Donald of Gaul, that's who. Right there in the middle of it all, me, the most famous showman in the world.

66 I had to have them. I sent a messenger to get my lawyers in Rome to write up a contract, and I got my girl from Gomorrah to sweet talk Jesus and John and invite them back to my place in Caesarea. She had it all, let me tell you, she was a ten plus. What man could say no to *that*?

67 By the time I got back to Caesarea, the whole town was talking about these guys. Some believed it, and some didn't, but the story was fantastic—John was a prophet, and Jesus was the Son of God.

68 The traveling preacher racket is already a gold mine, it's pure gold. No one's as easy to con as a religious person. You can take them for everything they own, or ten percent—they call it "tithing," these Jews—ten percent at the very least, that's what they tell me. It's like a protection racket, give me ten percent of everything you've got, and you won't get hurt.

69 And a little bit of magic doesn't hurt, either, the old hocus pocus. Only in the traveling preacher racket, it's not just a magic trick, it's called a miracle. Magicians are a denarius a dozen, but miracle workers, that's a rare breed.

70 Magic, religion, what's the difference? It doesn't matter to me, it doesn't matter at all, as long as it sells.

71 One way or another, I was going to get these guys under contract and make a fortune. I had to have them.

72 And when Donald of Gaul wants something, he gets it. One way or another.

2 Nobody else will talk about it, the fake scribes won't even touch it. But I'm pretty sure John the Batshit and Jesus had a secret, a really, *really* big secret. I mean, the biggest secret. A family secret.

2 I heard this stuff on the downlow from a few of the twelve apostles who worked with Jesus, and from some apostles who came along later, like Paul and Luke. I talked to them all, I was right there in the middle of it.

3 And they liked to talk, I have to tell you, they liked to talk, especially that Peter, or Simon, or whatever the hell his name was. Never could make up his mind what his name was, that Peter, or Simon. And Jesus called him "Cephas," but I'll get to that later, too. I figured he was on the lam. He had these aliases, after all.

4 You might ask, so what? Who doesn't have an alias or two at one point or another? Me included, I've called myself a miller, I've called myself a baron, whatever it takes. So I call him Aint Peter, as in, "That ain't Peter, it's someone else."

5 I hate to say it, in fact I won't say it, but really, they were losers, these apostles, all of them, except maybe Luke. I'll get to him later, too. Think about it, these apostles, they had Jesus, the best performer in the empire. And what did they do? Half of them wound up hanging from trees, or crucified upside down on crosses, or beheaded, or broke nobodies.

6 They could've been rich, they could've been winners, like me. I'm a winner, I win, win, win. I almost get sick and tired of winning, I win so much. But they were losers, total losers.

7 Back to the secret, which maybe I heard from Luke, and maybe I didn't. I'm not saying. Anyway, thirty years or so before I met Jesus, there was this guy, Zacharias, he was a priest somewhere up in the hills. I don't know where, it doesn't matter, he was a hillbilly, okay?

8 And Zacharias, he had this wife, Elisabeth. They didn't have any children. I don't know why, that doesn't matter, either. Maybe his sling was out of stones, maybe her delta was dried up, who knows.

9 They were old, as I understand it, I mean, really, really old. Anyway, he probably hadn't touched her in years. When all of a sudden, she shows up pregnant. Knocked up, a ciabatta in the oven, preggo, eating for due, a pisetto in the pod. You get the picture.

10 Now if I was Zacharias, I'd be wondering what the hell just happened. If they weren't my stones that did the deed, whose were they?

11 He was worried, he must have been, because Zacharias, he kept her hidden away for five or six months, and he didn't speak a word to anyone. I don't just mean he didn't speak a word about the baby, I mean he didn't speak any words at all. It was like he was struck dumb, totally dumb.

12 Six months later, this young girl shows up at Zacharias's house. Her name was Mary, she was Elizabeth's younger cousin. She was a virgin, she said, and she was engaged. And *she* was pregnant, too! Talk about a pickle! How the hell do you explain *that*? A pregnant, engaged *virgin*?

13 So Mary, she heads for the hills and moves in with the old folks, this Zacharias and Elisabeth, and leaves her fiancé back in Nazareth. Joseph was his name, this fiancé, and he must have known something was up, just like Zacharias did. But he lets her go, and they stay engaged. What a sissy, this Joseph, he was pathetic. Very low energy, that's what people tell me.

14 According to this apostle, I'm not saying which one, as soon as this Mary shows up and says "Howdy" to Elizabeth, Elizabeth's baby starts jumping around and turning cartwheels in her belly. And Elizabeth supposedly says to Mary—it sounds like a script again, I'm telling you—"Blessed are you among women, and blessed is the fruit of your womb."

15 And then, according to this apostle, Mary says, "My soul does magnify the Lord, and my spirit has rejoiced in God my Saviour." I mean, who talks like that? Like I said, Jesus and these apostles, they were all working from a script.

16 So get this, there they are, an old lady, all dried up and childless, and a young girl who hasn't been with a man yet, and they're cousins, and they're both pregnant and living in the same house.

17 What are the chances? I'm no doctor, but I can put two and two together. Something funny was going on, some kind of monkey business, if you know what I mean. And if I can put two and two together, anyone can do it. People must have been talking, people always talk.

18 Three months later, Elisabeth spits out a little boy. Eight days after that, according to their Jewish law, they go to circumscribe the boy—they were Jews, you know, real savages—so they go to circumscribe the boy, and they go to name him, what else? Zacharias, after the father, right?

19 But Elisabeth says, "No way, Jose, his name is John." And Zacharias, who hasn't spoken for nine months now, sits down at a table and writes, "Yep, name's John, alright." And presto, Zacharias can speak again, just like that.

20 I know it sounds crazy, but remember, this whole Jesus story, it was all a put on, a setup, a scam. A big-league hoax. And whoever wrote the script—I think I know who wrote it—he was fantastic, believe me.

21 Talk about a story, you have to hear this one about how John got his name. Zacharias, he tells everybody that right before he was struck dumb, this guy comes into the Temple and says his name is Gabriel, and he's an angel. Talk about nerve! An angel! I wish I'd thought of it, I bet angels can get away with anything.

22 This Gabriel, he says to Zacharias, "Your wife, Elisabeth, shall bear you a son, and you shall call his name JOHN. And he shall be filled with the Holy Ghost, even from his mother's womb. And many of the children of Israel shall he turn to the Lord their God, to make ready a people prepared for the Lord."

23 So that's the story of the birth of John the Batshit, angel and all, and how he was supposedly born to be a prophet. That's what the shills were talking about at the Jordan River, see, like it was all planned by this God of the Jews, Yahweh, that I call NoWay. What an angle, what a gimmick! It was brilliant, absolutely brilliant.

24 Now you're probably wondering where Mary went, because she left Zacharias's house right before John was born. Well, her story sounds pretty familiar if you ask me. It goes like this:

25 About three months after Elisabeth got knocked up, this same guy, Gabriel, comes up to Mary and tells *her* that he's an angel. I've called plenty of women angels, but I never thought of claiming to be one myself. Pretty slick, let me tell you, pretty slick.

26 So he says, "Hail, you that are highly favoured, the Lord is with you: blessed are you among women."

27 Now *that's* an opening line! I have a few of my own—"Hey, why don't you check out this scroll in my pocket?" Or, "Hey, you wanna come back to my palace and sit on my throne?" Kind of blunt, I know, but this Gabriel, he was smooth.

28 Mary, she was just a girl. You can understand that she was freaked out, totally freaked out. So this Gabriel, he says, "Fear not, Mary: For you have found favor with God. And, behold, you shall bring forth a son, and shall call his name JESUS.

29 He shall be great, and shall be called the Son of the Highest: and the Lord God shall give to him the throne of his father David: And he shall reign over the house of Jacob forever; and of his kingdom there shall be no end."

30 Now if you know anything about the Jews, well, their mothers, they push their sons real hard, make them work like hell. You have to be a doctor, or a lawyer, or a senator, or a prefect. And if a Jew boy disappoints his mother, good golly, you don't want to be around, that's what they tell me.

31 So Gabriel tells her, look, your son is going to rule over Israel, he's going to be the King of the Jews, forever. Genius! I wish I'd thought of it when I was in Judea. What a way to get some!

32 But this Mary, she's still freaked out, you can just imagine. She says, "How shall this be, seeing I know not a man?" Because she hadn't "known" this Joseph, if you know what I mean. He was a lot older than she was, very low energy, like I said, and they were waiting until they got hitched and all that. These Jews, they're so pious. It's a whole lot easier being a pagan.

33 Now Gabriel starts laying it on thick. He says, "The Holy Ghost shall come upon you, and the power of the Highest shall overshadow you: therefore also that holy thing which shall be born of you shall be called the Son of God. And, behold, your cousin, Elisabeth, she has also conceived a son in her old age; and this is the sixth month with her, who was called barren. For with God, nothing shall be impossible."

34 What a come on! I did your *cousin*, now let me do *you*! Well, whatever happened, happened, and like I said before, Mary winds up pregnant, and living with Zacharias and Elisabeth.

35 So what do you think happened? Maybe, just maybe, this Zacharias, he suddenly gets as potent as a racehorse and knocks up old Elisabeth. It's possible, I'm just saying, it's possible. But if you believe that, I have a bridge I want to sell you in a magical land across the sea.

36 And maybe, just maybe, this Mary, she's still a virgin and gets knocked up by the Holy Ghost. That's not a bad story, very creative, and what moxie! "I'm still a virgin, the Holy Ghost did it." It sure beats, "I was shtupping the gardener behind the barn."

37 Or maybe, just maybe, it's this Gabriel, see, that got both of them knocked up. He was there when it happened, not once, but twice. You do the

math. And then he named them both, he named them John and Jesus, I mean, who would do that except the father? And they were both short little guys, like, a head shorter than me, and they looked the same with the big noses and the long hair and the beards.

38 I have to give it to him, this Gabriel, he must've been slick. I'd pay him top denaro to teach me his tricks with the ladies, that I can tell you. I'd pay him well, very well.

39 So there you have it. Jesus and John were brothers, and their dad, this Gabriel, was a smooth operator. A damn good script writer, too, if you ask me. I wasn't born yesterday, I've been around. Gabriel wrote the whole thing.

40 I figure Gabriel taught them to hustle, too, like he hustled. And he must have taught them well, because they were the best. Not only that, they were the best magicians I'd ever seen, so he probably taught them their magic act, too.

41 Before long, people all over Judea and Samaria and Perea and Galilee believed that John was a prophet and Jesus was the Son of God and the King of the Jews.

42 Talk about a gold mine. No one's as gullible as a religious person, like I said, they're suckers. And Jesus and John, they had every holy roller in the eastern Mediterranean buzzing. A magician claiming to be the Son of God—what a way to run a scam! These traveling preachers, they have a hundred ways to get money off their marks.

43 I knew if I could sign Jesus and John to a contract, we could sell a million tickets all across the empire. My properties would be packed, I'd have the hottest act in the world. And they'd have to share the stage with me, Donald of Gaul.

44 I had to get in on it, I just had to.

3 There was a problem, though, right from the start, right from the day Jesus was born. And Jesus, he didn't want to deal with it. The "Son of God" thing was fantastic—talk about branding!—but the "King of the Jews" thing, it was dangerous.

2 Think about it. If you're the real King of the Jews, like Herod the Great was, or the Emperor of Rome, like Caesar Augustus was back then—and Rome owned the King of the Jews, see, like Rome owned every ruler in the empire—and some guy comes along saying *he's* the King of the Jews, what are you going to do? Get rid of him, right?

3 When you're on top, you can't let anyone mess with you, you can't let anyone show you up or put you down. Every king knows that, every emperor, hell, every gangster knows that. Nobody challenges the boss. If someone does, you have to get rid of him, it's that simple.

4 Anyway, the prophets had been saying for centuries that this new King of the Jews, this savior, was going to be born, and they claimed to know exactly where—in Bethlehem. It was a prophecy, the Jews loved those things, predicting the future and all.

5 Bethlehem was a little backwater in Judea, which is pretty much a shithole country if you ask me. And that's exactly where Jesus was born, in Bethlehem, in Judea, in a barn if you can believe it. So even before he was born, the Jews were stirring up trouble for Jesus by calling him the King of the Jews. Like I said, there was a problem, right from the start. Here's how it all happened:

6 Caesar Augustus, the emperor, he wanted to raise taxes. Always raising taxes, these people, and giving away the hard-earned money of the rich to losers all over the place. Let me tell you, folks, Rome lets everyone take advantage of her, the poor, the shithole countries, her allies, everyone. Taken advantage of by every nation in the world, virtually, taking care of every lowlife out there. It's out of control, totally out of control.

7 Anyway, Augustus, he made everyone go to their hometowns to be counted in a census. It wasn't *really* to be counted in a census, it was to be *taxed*. But that's how he did it, because he was smart, very smart. Not as smart as me, I'm, like, *really* smart. But he was smart, very smart.

8 And so Joseph, the one who left Mary knocked up at Zacharias's house—I call him Low Energy Joseph—he took her to Bethlehem, because his family was from Bethlehem. So they went to Bethlehem, with Mary as big as a house.

9 And wouldn't you know it, the inn was full, there was no room at the inn. "No Vacancy." Unbelievable. Didn't they ever hear of reservations? That Low Energy Joseph, what a lightweight. A very low-IQ person, a real loser. He should have had a reservation.

10 So what do they do? You won't believe this, but they hole up in a barn! Or a stable, whatever, I don't know the difference, I'm not a hillbilly. What's the difference, they're both full of vermin. It's disgusting.

11 And that's where Mary gives birth, and they swaddle the kid up real tight in some sheets, and they stick him in a manger, of all things, right there in the stable with the pigs and the horses and the cows and the rats.

12 "The Virgin Mary," they call her. More like the Vermin Mary if you ask me. Such a nasty woman. Honestly, she should be locked up, she should be. Lock her up, that's what I say, lock her up! What a disgrace.

13 Can you believe anyone would keep their kid like that, like it was an animal, in a pen, or a cage? Who the hell does that? Children in pens? Well, slaves' kids, maybe, or refugees' kids—hell, they probably belong in pens, why waste your money on them—but your own kid? Come on, it's terrible.

14 Now here's where it gets weird, depending on who you listen to. This apostle, Luke, he was a doctor, I mean a real doctor, not one of these faith healers out on the circuit. Luke tells me the story like this—you have to hear it, it's a real humdinger:

15 According to Luke, there were these shepherds outside of Bethlehem, and an angel—not Gabriel, he must've been busy—another angel comes down out of the sky.

16 This angel, he says to these shepherds, "Behold, I bring you good tidings of great joy, for to you is born this day in the city of David a Saviour, which is

Christ the Lord. And this shall be a sign to you: You shall find the babe wrapped in swaddling clothes, lying in a manger."

17 Then a whole host of angels starts singing, "Glory to God in the highest, Peace on earth, Good will toward men." It sounds like a musical, doesn't it? Great scriptwriter, and a lyricist to boot, that Gabriel. I'd hire him just like that to write for my theaters.

18 Like I said before, when the Jews say someone's the Son of God, they mean the only son of the only God, Yahweh, that I call NoWay. And "Christ the Lord," for the Jews, that was the top banana, big time, the messiah. If you could make people believe *that*, you'd have them in the palm of your hand.

19 Anyway, according to Luke, these shepherds, well, of course, they go into Bethlehem, because that was the city of David. Before you know it, they find this kid, wrapped in sheets, lying in a manger. I mean, how many could there be? How many parents would do that to a kid?

20 These shepherds, they start running around telling everyone about the angel, and the manger, and the baby, and that he's Christ the Lord.

21 Eight days later, being Jews, they take the kid, Jesus, to Jerusalem to be circumscribed. And some old priest, Simeon was his name, he sees this Jesus, and right away he gives a speech.

22 This Simeon, he figures he's ready to die now that he's seen Jesus. He says, "Lord, now let your servant depart in peace, according to your word: For mine eyes have seen thy salvation, which you have prepared before the face of all people, a light to lighten the gentiles, and the glory of your people Israel."

23 Well, you'd think one prophet was enough. But Luke piles it on thick. There was this old woman, Anna, she was a prophetess, and she goes to see this Jesus there in Jerusalem, like she was drawn to him. And right away, *she* says the same schtick!

24 So according to Luke, not one, but *two* prophets called Jesus the messiah and the King of the Jews, just as soon as he was born. And then, according to

Luke, Low Energy Joseph, he takes Mary and Jesus, and they high tail it back to Nazareth.

25 But Luke wasn't the only one telling the story. There was this other guy, Matthew—I'll get to him later—he was a tax collector for the Romans. What a job that must have been. I mean, who's going say no to a Roman tax collector, unless you want to be crucified, am I right?

26 Well Matthew, he tells me a story twice as good as Luke's. But that's where the problem comes in, because in Matthew's story, my friend Herod the Great—the real King of the Jews and a good buddy of Augustus Caesar—finds out all about Jesus before he's even born, and naturally, he wants the kid dead.

27 So according to Matthew, when Jesus was born, these three wise men from the east come to Jerusalem by following a star. Yeah, that's right, they followed a star. And they say, "Hey, we hear there's a new King of the Jews that was just born. We followed this here star to find him."

28 By the way, what kind of job is "wise man?" I mean, how do you make a shekel just by being wise? They sound lazy to me, and worthless, these wise men, like teachers and writers. And what about this star? If these guys could make a star appear above Jesus, maybe they could put stars above my Donald Baths, or my Donald Inns, or my Donald Theaters. That would bring them in, I'd make a fortune!

29 Anyway, according to Matthew, these wise men weren't there by coincidence. Even before Jesus was born, my friend Herod the Great had gotten wind of it, so he called out all the priests and scribes, and he said, where's this Christ fella gonna to be born?

30 And the priests and scribes looked at all the old prophets—these Jews, they had more prophets than you could shake a stick at, I'm telling you—and they said, he's going to be born in Bethlehem, in Judea. So Herod tells these three wise men, hey, go check out Bethlehem. And if you find the kid, let me know, I wanna go worship him.

31 The wise men, they follow this star, and they go to Bethlehem, and they find the same thing the shepherds found: Low Energy Joseph, the Vermin Mary,

and little Jesus all wrapped in sheets in a manger in a pig pen in a barn. Or a stable, or whatever, I don't know about all that, except that there must be a lot of fertilizer laying around, if you know what I mean.

32 These wise men, I figure two of them were pretty wise, but the third one must've been kind of stupid if you ask me. The first wise man, he gives the baby some frankincense, which smells great. A nice gift when you're changing diapers, especially when you're surrounded by animals and all that fertilizer.

33 The second one, he gives the baby some myrrh, which is some good oil, some of the best. Another nice gift, perfect for diaper rash.

34 The third, he gives the baby some gold. Gold? Really? That's pretty rich for a baby that you don't even know. Why not a dreidel, or a rattle, or some other toy? So this third wise man, maybe he wasn't so wise, maybe he was pretty dopey.

35 Anyway, here's where it gets interesting. First, the wise men, they have a dream, and this Jew god NoWay tells them, forget Herod, he's up to no good. Go on home, don't tell Herod a thing. They do that, these wise men, they go on home and leave Herod looking like a schmuck.

36 Then an angel comes to Joseph and says, forget Nazareth, hightail it down to Egypt. Herod wants the kid dead, you have to take a powder. Joseph does that, he heads for Egypt with his wife and baby.

37 Sure enough, when the wise men don't show up, Herod gets pissed, I mean, really pissed. He sits around all pissed off for a while, then he sends his soldiers to Bethlehem with orders to kill, and they kill all the boys that are two years old or younger. And not just in Bethlehem, but all over that shithole country, right up and down the coast.

38 I have to say, I sort of admire Herod, it took guts to do that. Because you have to be strong, you have to protect yourself no matter what. Believe me, if you're a big shot, everyone wants a piece of you.

39 So Low Energy Joseph and the Vermin Mary, they wait it out in Egypt, and then another angel comes to Joseph—these Jews and their angels, holy moly—and he tells Joseph to go on home to Judea.

40 By now, my friend Herod is dead, and his deadbeat son, Archelaus, is in charge. I call him Archelaus the Deadbeat, I knew him, too, he was nothing like his father. But Joseph doesn't trust this boy, Archelaus the Deadbeat, any more than he did the father, Herod the Great, so he hides out in a little hick town out in the desert.

41 Eventually Archelaus gets the boot, he gets kicked out of the empire and sent to Gaul, where I'm from. And his little brother Herod Antipas becomes king. I knew Herod Antipas, too, he wasn't a bad guy, but that fig fell pretty far from the tree. He wound up getting kicked out of the empire, just like his brother. Poor Herod, not one, but two worthless sons, can you imagine?

42 Anyway, according to Matthew, Joseph says, "Whew," and he takes Mary and Jesus and heads on home to Nazareth, and they set up shop as carpenters. Made a pretty good living, they tell me, building houses and doing renovations and making crosses for the Romans.

43 So that's Matthew's story. Two stories, one according to Luke, and one according to Matthew. They can't both be right, can they? Maybe Luke is right, maybe Matthew is right, maybe they're both full of camel patties. Who knows. If I had to pick one story, I'd go with Matthew's. When in doubt, just go with the better story, okay? The one that gets the job done.

44 Well, nobody seems to know much about Jesus as a kid. But there's this one story, it's another one of Luke's, and it's pretty good, too. It goes like this:

45 Low Energy Joseph and the Vermin Mary, they get into the habit of going to Jerusalem for the Passover. This Passover, it's some kind of Jewish holiday. Let me tell you, they have as many holidays as us pagans do, these Jews. I don't know much about it, this Passover, but it doesn't sound like much fun to me.

46 When Jesus was twelve, Joseph and Mary had just finished their Passover vacation and left Jerusalem. Halfway to Nazareth, they realize, where the hell is Jesus? Nobody knows! They lost the kid! Talk about low energy, what the hell was Joseph thinking? Talk about vermin, what kind of mother loses her kid?

47 So they head back to Jerusalem, and they look all over the place trying to find Jesus. And what do you know, after three days going all over town, they finally find him in the Temple. He's sitting there talking with the priests and doctors, and he knows more than any of them, and they're all speechless.

48 You can imagine, The Vermin Mary was freaking out. Remember what I said about Jewish mothers? Oy vey! (That's how they say, "Holy cow!") Mary lights into the boy, she says, "Son, why have you thus dealt with us? Behold, your father and I have sought you in sorrowing."

49 Jesus, he gives as good as he takes. He says back, **How is it that you sought me? Knew you not that I must be about my father's business?** His *father's* business! That would be Gabriel, like I said. And there's Low Energy Joseph standing right there, the idiot, not knowing what the hell Jesus is talking about.

50 His "father's business." I figure by then, Jesus knew that Gabriel was his real father, and he was learning some magic and some faith healing and some traveling preacher type stuff behind Joseph's back. He knew even then that he was going into the traveling preacher business. I mean, who wants to be a carpenter? It's damn hard work, and I should know, I hire them by the hundreds.

51 For the next couple of decades, nobody knows where Jesus was. Some people say he was traveling back east, or maybe he had a woman stashed some- where. I don't know, but I figure he was probably with his dad Gabriel and his brother John, learning their trade in the Orient. The best magicians, see, they're Orientals.

52 Jesus was about thirty when I met him, so John was thirty, thirty-one. And they were doing this traveling preacher thing and this Son of God thing like nobody's business. Gabriel must've taught them well, real well. Like I said before, I knew these guys were good, real good—they were the best magicians ever—and I wanted them in my shows.

53 But there was a problem, like I also said, right from the day Jesus was born. Here's the problem: King Herod had wanted this kid dead. Well, King

Herod was gone by now, and his first son, Archelaus the Deadbeat, was gone, too.

54 So now, Herod's second son, Herod Antipas, is in charge. I called him Herod Antipasto, like the appetizer. He didn't think it was funny, but what the hell, what was he going to do? I was a friend of his father's, he had to show me some respect.

55 Caesar Augustus, he was gone by then, too. Now Tiberius Caesar was the one in charge in Rome, and Herod Antipasto was like a little lap dog to Tiberius.

56 But don't you know, these guys at the top, they have long memories. They have to. And not everyone had forgotten about the so-called King of the Jews that was born in Bethlehem, not even after Herod killed all those kids. You can't be too careful, know what I mean? And the kings' counsellors, they had long memories, too, that was their job.

57 The Jews, the Romans—as soon as Jesus stuck his head up into the limelight, which he was just about to do after that act at the Jordan River, he was going to get burned. King of the Jews, Son of God, he might as well put a target on his back. I couldn't have that.

58 So here's what I did. First, I spread the word that Jesus was born in Nazareth, not Bethlehem. I told everyone I could, I even paid off some fake scribes to write it down. I sent out the word, forget what anyone says, Jesus was born in Nazareth.

59 How does anyone really know where a guy was born anyway? You can say anything, who's going to know any different? The truth doesn't matter, it's the story that gets the job done that matters.

60 I made it real simple, too; I just made sure everyone I knew called him "Jesus of Nazareth." Three simple words. Branding 101. Before you know it, just about everyone was calling him "Jesus of Nazareth," like that had always been his name. Mission accomplished.

61 But that wasn't enough. I figured, the best defense is a good offense. So I spread another rumor that King Herod, the first one, Herod the Great, was

born in Babylon. Babylon! That would make him and his sons Babylonians, and the Jews hate the Babylonians, they hate their guts.

62 I sent out my best undercover men to investigate where Herod was born, on the downlow, asking questions all over Judea. I had all the scribes and town criers talking about it. I paid a bunch of priests and rabbis to spread the rumor, and before you know it, it's all that people were talking about.

63 This Herod Antipasto, I knew him, like I said, I knew him well. I helped him build Tiberias, his capital on the Sea of Galilee—he named it after his boss, Tiberius Caesar, he knew which side his bread was buttered on. And I helped him build a wall around Beth-Aram, which was right around the corner from Jericho. It was one hell of a wall, much better than the one built by those losers at Jericho.

64 Anyway, the last thing Herod Antipasto, the King of the Jews, wanted was for his people to think he was a Babylonian. I figured, there's no way this guy's going to say a word about Jesus being born in Bethlehem, when that would get everyone talking about his own dad being born in Babylon.

65 It's all about the words, using the best words, the ones that hit people in the gut. "Babylon," that one really gets your goat if you're a Jew.

66 If you say something often enough, people will start to believe it, especially if it's something they want to believe. That's the trick, see—tell people what they want to hear, and you can get them to buy anything. If you're going to make a story stick, you have to make it simple. Tell them what they want to hear, hit them in the gut, make it simple, and say it over and over and over again.

67 So Jesus was born in Nazareth, and Herod the Great was from Babylon. Problem solved, by me, Donald of Gaul, at least for a while.

68 If Jesus had just listened to me, he would've been in the clear. But he didn't, and before long, he wasn't; but I'll get to that later.

4 Back to the story. When John baptized Jesus, and they did that magic trick with the sunbeams and the dove and the thunder and the voice of God, I knew I had to sign them up pronto. But this Jesus, what does he do? Take advantage of the opportunity? Strike while the iron is hot? No, he decides to go camping.

2 Camping! Seriously, who goes camping at a time like that? But he said he had to spend forty days and forty nights in the wilderness, fasting. Yeah, fasting! He was already skinny as a rail, why the hell would he want to fast?

3 Great Jupiter, he should've been out there branding and promoting, promoting and branding. That's how you sell tickets, that's how you start scamming the peasants and the zealots. But camping? Fasting? And forty days and forty nights? Why forty?

4 I could've talked him out of it, but he wouldn't come to Caesarea, not even with my secretary from Gomorrah using all her charms, and they were some kind of charms, I can tell you that.

5 Neither would John. He went right back to the river for more preaching and dunking, dunking and preaching. Why did he have to do it in that river, the Jordan, anyway? It was a sewer, a real sewer. Why not come to my Donald Bath in Rome, or any of my bath houses, and get in on the wet tunic contests?

6 A little preaching, a little magic, that's fine, but wet tunics, that's what sells tickets. But these guys, they never sold a single ticket. They didn't take a plug quadrans from anybody at any of their shows as far as I could tell. What the hell? Who works for free? Nobody, that's who. They were up to something, but I couldn't figure out what.

7 Well, as soon as my secretary from Gomorrah told me that Jesus and John weren't coming to Caesarea, I sent my best men out into the wilderness to find Jesus. And wouldn't you know it, they couldn't find him for weeks and weeks. It was like he disappeared off the face of the earth.

8 Then, finally, they find him and his campsite, out in the Judean Desert between Jerusalem and the Dead Sea. So I take my chariot out to see him. He was a mess, you should have seen this guy. Dirty, smelly, skinny, bags under

his eyes, like some homeless person, some bum. He looked as bad as John the Batshit—pathetic, a total disaster.

9 I brought him a new robe, a silk robe to be exact, the best silk money could buy. And some nice boots, leather boots, made of the best leather from Hispania. But he wouldn't take them! And I brought him food, the best food, and wine, the best Falernian wine, but he wouldn't eat anything or touch the wine.

10 I didn't blame him about the wine. I never touch the stuff, but my people, the Gauls, they drink it like water. But the food and the clothes? It was like he *wanted* to suffer, he wanted to look poor.

11 I figured, maybe he learned this from some swami in the Orient. Those swamis, they do all kinds of crazy things, like standing on one leg on top of a pole, or measuring China using their own bodies, or burying themselves up to their necks and living off water from a straw. Like suffering makes them seem more holy, if you can believe that. It's a tough racket, the swami thing.

12 Or maybe it was part of a magic trick, some promotion that he didn't want to let me in on. Maybe there was something he was planning with John the Batshit, and he had to look like that to pull it off, but it didn't make any sense to me.

13 I finally get out to see the guy, and I'm thinking of his magic act and what we could sell across the empire, and I'm looking at him sitting there half-starved and half naked. It was like he'd forgotten all about his magic. But I wanted him thinking about his act, his career. You have to keep your focus, right?

14 So I look around, and I say, "Hey Jesus, why don't you turn those stones over there into loaves of bread? You must be hungry as hell, you're really hungry, aren't you?" *That* would be some kind of a trick, and it would make sense after all that fasting, turning rocks into bread and all.

15 But no, Jesus, he wasn't much of a self-promoter. He just said, and it was in this meek little voice he usually used, **It is written, That man shall not live by bread alone, but by every word of God.**

16 Well, I'd hate to live off bread alone myself, you have to eat, right? I have the best cooks money can buy, I eat like a king. I know my way around a vomitorium, that I can tell you. But what the hell was he talking about? You can't eat words, even the best words, which are mine, like I said before.

17 Then I take him up a mountain, and I show him this fantastic view, it's just incredible. And I say, "Hey Jesus, sign up with me, and I could give you all of this, every last bit of it. I mean, it's kind of a shithole country, but just think of the acreage! It would all be yours, as far as the eye can see."

18 But no, Jesus wasn't into real estate. He just says, with that same sad smile of his, **Get you behind me, Donald; for it is written, You shall worship the Lord your God, and him only shall you serve.**

19 Now I was getting a little tired of all that "God" schtick. I get it, I get it, you're playing the Son of God. Great idea, great branding, the best! But it's me, Donald of Gaul, I'm trying to do some business here!

20 So I pull out all the stops, okay? I take him back to Jerusalem, and I take him to the Temple, and up the highest tower in the place, and I say, "Hey Jesus, here's a trick for you. Jump off this tower, and do your hocus pocus, and have some angels pop up and flutter you down to the ground. That'll get the people buzzing, they'll eat it up!"

21 But no, Jesus wasn't ready for another show just yet. He just says, kind of shaking his head, **It is said, You shall not tempt the Lord your God.**

22 Then I laid it on the line. I asked him, I practically begged him, to sign a contract with me. He and John the Batshit, an exclusive deal to work my Donald properties all over the Mediterranean, all over the Roman Empire. I offered him a million sesterces to split with his brother John any way he wanted.

23 That's right, I offered him a *million sesterces*, a cool million! He just shook his head and smiled that sad smile of his, and then he turned around and walked away. He walked away from me, Donald of Gaul. I have to tell you, I was starting to wonder if this guy was nuts. I mean, I could've made him the biggest thing in the whole empire. I could've booked him at the Circus Maximus, he could've been a superstar.

24 But that wasn't the worst of it. My people, they come and tell me there's another problem: Herod Antipasto has put John the Batshit in prison. Seems John had been badmouthing Antipasto all over Galilee and Perea after Antipasto married his brother Philip's wife.

25 Come on, wives are as cheap as cattle. You wear one out, you get a new one. She gets old, you find a young one. It's like a chariot as far as I'm concerned—you get sick of one, you trade it in on a new model.

26 Anyway, Antipasto had married this woman, Herodias. She'd been his brother Philip's wife before, so she was also his niece. And John, he said hey, that's pretty perverted, us being Jews and all, we're supposed to be all pious, not like these Romans and pagans.

27 That pissed Antipasto off, I mean, bigly, he was really pissed. And John was already causing trouble by stirring up all these Jews with his preaching, and the Jews, they were always making trouble for the Romans to begin with. Not to mention, John was calling Jesus the King of the Jews, when everyone knew the King of the Jews was Herod Antipasto.

28 Then Herodias' daughter, Salome was her name—she was one hot little number, I moved on her very heavily, I moved on her like a bitch, but I couldn't get there—she was at Antipasto's birthday party. And he liked them young, I mean, who doesn't, am I right?

29 So he tells Salome he'll give her anything she wants—anything—if she'll dance at his party. She dances, and it must have been some kind of dance, because when she was done, and Antipasto was all worked up, she says, "So, Antipas, I want John the Baptist's head on a platter."

30 Herod Antipasto, he couldn't say no to a juicy little number like that. So bing, bang, bong! Off goes John's head, and this girl Salome, she gets it on a platter, just like that.

31 Anyway, Jesus, now he's lost his sidekick. And it was his brother, and they were both trained by their father Gabriel, and they had their schtick down pat. So what does he do?

32 I have to give him credit. Jesus, he doesn't give up easy. No, not at all. He goes down to the Sea of Galilee—these beach towns, they're always ripe for a good show—and on the way he starts preaching in the synagogues, and doing his act all over the place, until he has the people really buzzing again.

33 I tell him, now *that's* the way to work it! He was getting famous, really famous, even more famous than John the Batshit. He was working the traveling preacher circuit like a pro.

34 But that wasn't all. Jesus, he starts this faith healer routine. Everywhere he goes, he's healing the blind, and healing people with the palsy, and healing lepers. More shills, I figured. And easy, too, I mean, how hard is it to fake being blind?

35 Or how hard is it to fake a palsy? I've done it myself. One time, in a speech at one of my rallies, I made fun of this spastic scribe who called me a liar. Yeah, he called me a liar, the scumbag. Then he denied it, the sleazeball, he denied calling me a liar!

36 You should have seen it, I started shaking and throwing my arms all around like a spaz, and I said, "The poor guy, you've got to see this guy," and I started moaning and gurgling and talking like he talked. "Ahhhhgh, I don't know what I said, ahhhhgh, I don't remember." It was hilarious, you should have seen it.

37 Leprosy, that one's tougher to fake, and more dramatic, way more dramatic. That takes some doing, like, some top-notch makeup work. I figured they had some theater people making these shills up like lepers.

38 So what did I do? I got my best make-up people to come over from Rome, and we worked up this fake leprosy cream, and we hired actors to run all up and down Judea and Galilee following Jesus around and pretending to be lepers. When Jesus comes along, they run up and touch his robe, or beg him for a healing. Bing bang bong, they wipe off the cream, and presto! They're healed.

39 Believe me, things started popping. This one shill, he's acting like a leper—maybe he was one of ours, maybe he wasn't, I don't know—he sees Jesus,

and he falls flat on his face, and he starts begging like crazy, "Lord, if you will, you can make me clean!"

40 Now that's a shill that's worth his weight in gold! You have to sell it, trust me, you have to sell it. Jesus, he puts out his hand and touches this guy, and he says, **I will. Be you clean.** Presto, no more leprosy.

41 Then he tells this guy, **See you say nothing to any man: but go your way, show yourself to the priest, and offer for your cleansing those things which Moses commanded, for a testimony to them.**

42 Now, I don't get all that gobbledygook about Moses, that Jew prophet stuff, but that bit about "Say nothing to any man" was clever, really clever. "Don't tell anyone, especially not the priest!" Right, he might as well have said, "Tell everyone, and do it now, starting with the priest!" And that's exactly what this guy did, he told everyone he could find, just like Jesus wanted. Word of mouth, it's the best advertising.

43 Well the people, they ate it up alright, they loved the faith healing. More and more of them started flocking to see Jesus do his schtick. In fact, he could barely move around, there were so many people coming to see him. He was mobbed everywhere he went, absolutely mobbed.

44 He was no slouch, this Jesus. He knew how to put on a show. He was in this one house—I was right there—he was surrounded by fans, and some guys were trying to carry their buddy with the palsy in on a sofa for a healing. But there were so many people there, they couldn't get through the door.

45 So, what do they do? They climb onto the roof, and they lower this guy, sofa and all, into the house through a hole in the roof. Talk about showmanship! Jesus, he puts on that sad smile, and in that meek little voice of his, he says to this guy, **Man, your sins are forgiven you.**

46 There were these scribes and Pharisees there that day. *Fake* scribes, I should say, and these Pharisees, they were all uppity and self-righteous, you know the type. Just looking to judge you. And they're making faces at him, they're all, like, who's this Jesus to forgive sins? Who does he think he is?

47 Jesus, he knows what these scribes and Pharisees are thinking, so he says, **What reason you in your hearts? Whether it is easier to say, Your sins be forgiven you; or to say, Rise up and walk?** He says this to the fake scribes and the Pharisees, right to their faces.

48 Then he says, **But that you may know that the Son of man has power on earth to forgive sins...** He pauses, real dramatic like, and he looks at the guy with the palsy, and he says, **I say to you, Arise, and take up your couch, and go into your house.**

49 Sure enough, the guy hops up and grabs that sofa, and off he goes, sofa and all. What a show that was! Not just a healing, but Jesus, he shows up those fake scribes and those snooty Pharisees to boot. Nobody likes a goody two shoes. I loved it, and the people, they loved it, too.

50 Word was getting out that Jesus was a must-see act, the biggest thing in the eastern Mediterranean. He was on fire, like, big league. And from there, who knows? He could've toured the whole empire, and taken Rome by storm, that's what he could've done.

51 It was time to cash in, nobody knew that better than I did. I still hadn't signed Jesus to a contract, but my people, they were all over him with offers, and swag, and girls. But nothing seemed to get to this guy, it was like he didn't care about money, or fame. But everyone wants money, we all know that, and this guy Jesus, he wanted fame, he wanted it bad.

52 I still couldn't figure out his angle. He had to have a side hustle somewhere, he had to have a way to cash in. I needed an angle of my own, I had to get through to this guy.

53 And then, bam! It hit me. He needed a new sidekick. A good magician always has a sidekick. John the Batshit was one helluva sidekick, but he was dead, and he wasn't coming back from a beheading. No one, no magician anywhere, is *that* good.

54 Well I had a plan to find Jesus the best sidekick in the Roman Empire, and a sidekick that would be my man on the inside, too.

55 It was a perfect plan, it couldn't miss.

5 So here was my plan, and it was amazing. You put out the word that a big-name magician is looking for some assistants, see? And the assistants are going to be big, I mean, really big, like, world famous.

2 Then you get a couple hundred guys and girls who want the gig, and you weed out the ugly ones, the dumb ones, and the losers. You want them to be winners, and you want them to be smart. And you want them to be good looking, they should all be good looking, like my secretaries. That's how you sell tickets, a little eye candy never hurt anyone.

3 Now you get it down to, say, two or three dozen, and you put them in a competition, like a talent show. I had the best talent shows in my theaters, the very best, we sold them out all over the empire. Only, talent shows are for amateurs, but this is for real, a real gig. It's theater, but it's also reality, okay? I call it "reality theater." What a concept!

4 And talent shows are local, right? They're in big towns and small towns and everything in between, but they're local. Except this time, you put the show on the road, touring all the best Donald properties in the empire, and everywhere you go, you send criers and scribes out ahead to drum up the business.

5 You get a few new contestants at every town, and you keep a few, and you dump a few. So it's not just local anymore, it's all over the empire.

6 That's not all. You let it get ugly, real ugly, maybe even a fight here and there. The people, they love a good fight, they love competition. They love backstabbing, gladiators get stabbed in the back all the time, and it's a big draw. They'd love to see the losers get kicked out, too, as long as it hurts. The more it hurts, the better. Bring out the worst in people, that's what you do.

7 The whole time, you're heading for Rome, the Circus Maximus, for the final show where you pick one guy to be the sidekick, and a few good-looking

guys and gals to be assistants—magicians always have assistants, good-looking ones, right there on stage, everyone knows that.

8 And I wasn't just going to *bankroll* the show, I was going to be the *star*. Me, Donald of Gaul, right there on the stage, running the whole show. My name all over the place, in letters ten cubits tall! I mean, why not, I already draw the biggest crowds ever, absolutely the biggest.

9 At every show, I'd pick the winners and the losers. Imagine it, the whole Roman Empire hanging on my every word. You're in, you're a winner, come on over. You're out, you're a loser, you're fired. Who wouldn't want to see *that*? "You're fired," such beautiful words, I love to say them. Fired, fired, fired.

10 And the women—what a way to get women. So you want to be in *my* show? How about a little hanky panky, huh? Let me tell you, when you're famous like I am, you can get all the women you want. And even the ones you don't get, you can get a little action, you know, some smooching, cop a feel. When you're a star, they let you do it, you can do anything. Grab them by the delta, you can do anything, it's fantastic.

11 Anyway, I had it all planned out. So I go to Jesus, and I pitch the plan, and I tell him he's going to be the biggest thing in the Roman Empire. A new sidekick, some assistants, money, girls, people taking care of his every need. Standing dates at the best Donald properties all over the empire. The works.

12 This time, I bring him another contract, and I offer him ten million sesterces. *Ten million sesterces,* can you believe it? Who could say no to ten million?

13 So what does he do? He gives me that sad smile of his, he shakes his head, and he walks away. Just like that, he walks away, he doesn't say a word.

14 He goes back down to the Sea of Galilee, and I've had it with him, so I decide to go to Jerusalem for a while to do some business. I still had my people on him, they reported everything he did back to me. I wasn't giving up, but I had business to do, I wanted to expand past Jerusalem into the whole eastern Mediterranean.

15 I was worth four, maybe six billion sesterces back then, and sesterces, they don't grow on trees. I was big back in Avaricum, and in Rome, and I had businesses in Hispania, Britannia, even Carthage. But I wanted to expand and keep moving east, putting "Donald" on buildings in every town that was worth the trouble.

16 Besides, I figured it wouldn't hurt to get myself known in Jerusalem. That's where the Jews did all their business, and they're some great businessmen, let me tell you. They even did business in the Temple, and I wanted to make connections there, too, even if it meant putting on a yarmulke and banging my head on a Torah.

17 I told this one bunch of Jews, I said, "Look, I'm a negotiator like you folks, we're negotiators. This room negotiates perhaps more than any room I've spoken to, maybe more. The only bad news is, I can't get you on Saturday." Saturday, that's their Sabbath day, they don't work on the Sabbath. So that was a little joke, and Jews love jokes. They're not just great businessmen, they're the best comedians, too, the very best.

18 So I went to the synagogues, and I prayed to their little god Yahweh, and I got baptized and fasted and gave alms to the poor. You know, the whole Jew rigamarole, right down to the yarmulke.

19 I do the same thing with the pagans in Rome, go to all their feasts and festivals, pray to their little gods in their little temples, I drink my little wine and eat my little crackers, the works. You have to put on a show, I'm telling you. These people, if they're religious, they eat it up, and boy are they easy prey.

20 I don't know how he did it, but by then, Jesus had people following him by the thousands, that's what people were telling me. Not as many as I had, nobody has bigger crowds than me, but still, pretty good, he was okay. He had so many people following him around that he couldn't hardly find a place to perform.

21 But he was pretty sharp, he always found a way to get in front of a crowd. This one time, he was down by the Sea of Galilee, and he was being mobbed by

these fans. So he found this guy, he was a Jew fisherman, and he says to the guy, let me in your boat, then push off a little and let me do my act from your boat.

22 The guy with the boat, it turns out it was Simon, or Peter, or whatever the hell his name was—I call him Aint Peter, like I said—Aint Peter, he pushes off, and Jesus starts preaching up a storm.

23 This Aint Peter, he was a loser, I can tell you that. His nets were empty, totally empty. Some fisherman, not a fish in the whole boat. So right in the middle of the act, Jesus tells him, **Launch out into the deep, and let down your nets for a catch.**

24 He had to be on the lam, Aint Peter, or hiding from someone. Probably borrowed some money from the money lenders in the Temple. These Jews, they're tough when it comes to money, you don't want to be owing them money, no way. *Counting* your money and *lending* your money, that's what you want Jews for. All my money lenders are Jews, every one of them, and most of my money counters, too.

25 So anyway, Aint Peter throws his net over, and abracadabra! So many fish come up, the net starts to bust open. The next boat over, it was sailed by Aint Peter's partners, James and John, they were brothers. Aint Peter says, "Hey, how 'bout a little help!" And James and John, and Aint Peter's brother, Andrew, they pull up their nets and fill both boats with so many fish, they're ready to sink.

26 Now that's a magic trick, let me tell you. James and John and Andrew had to be in on it, of course. I didn't just fall off the turnip cart, they must've had some nets already full of fish underwater before Jesus came on board.

27 Well, the people, they went wild. They weren't just walking and riding donkeys to see Jesus anymore, they were coming in boats and caravans. Jesus, he's got the ball rolling, big time.

28 And now he has a new sidekick, Aint Peter, the so-called fisherman, and he has three new assistants, these other three fishermen. He must have listened to my advice about sidekicks and assistants after all, he just didn't want to let me in on it, at least not yet.

29 But these fishermen, Aint Peter and James and John and Andrew, they were new to show biz. Fish, they knew, and believe me, they knew fish. They smelled like fish all the time. I mean, get a little frankincense, am I right? But they didn't know show biz, and they were worried about making a living.

30 So Jesus, he tells Aint Peter, **Fear not; from now on, you shall be catching men.**

31 What a way to put it, "You shall be catching men!" I say to myself, now he's getting it, it's all about the words. The words are the bait. Use them right, and you can catch all the people you want.

32 Never mind fishing, that's a tough way to make a living, like carpentry. But the traveling preacher racket, that's more like spearing fish in a barrel. These religious nuts, they're suckers, patsies, easy marks, the easiest if you ask me. So I track Jesus down again, and I start telling him the tricks of the trade, thinking maybe that'll get him on board with me.

33 First, I say, you have to get the government in your back pocket. You can't do business without connections in the government, you have to have people on the inside. That's easy, you do some schmoozing, you grease some palms, you spread the money around real thick to every politician you can find. If you can't get rich dealing with politicians, there's something wrong with you, that I can tell you.

34 And what do you know, Jesus, he follows my advice again, he gets this new assistant, Matthew. This guy, Matthew, they also called him Levi, he was another Jew, but he worked as a tax collector for the Romans, like I said before. Mission accomplished, he's got a government guy on board.

35 So that's five assistants, only Jesus, he calls these guys "apostles." Great idea, if you're going play the faith healer and miracle worker angles, use the right words. Jesus Christ and the Apostles, now *that's* branding!

36 And I tell Jesus, keep it up, now you have to give these guys nicknames. What the hell, half of them have two names already anyhow. Everyone loves a nickname, it's the best kind of branding, I do it all the time.

37 He takes my advice again. He tells Aint Peter, **You are Simon the son of Jona; you shall be called Cephas. Upon this rock I will build my church: and the gates of hell shall not prevail against it.** "Cephas," that means "Stone." What a great nickname! It sounds tough, very tough.

38 He calls James and John, the brothers, he calls them James and John Boanerges. "Boanerges" means "The Sons of Thunder." I loved it! "The Sons of Thunder!" They could've been gladiators with a name like that. Not bad, I figured, when they get to Rome, they'll be ready set for the arenas.

39 And word starts to spread. Everyone is saying, you gotta go see these guys! Jesus Christ and the Apostles, they rock! Well, nothing succeeds better than success. Before you know it, three more apostles come on board, this guy Philip, and this guy Bartholomew, and this guy Thomas. That makes eight.

40 And they keep coming, these apostles. There was another guy named James, he was Matthew's brother, and another guy from Canaan named Simon, if you can believe it. Two Jameses and two Simons, that's bad for business, too confusing.

41 So what does Jesus do next? He gets two more guys with practically the same name, Jude Thaddaeus and Judas Iscariot. Can you believe it? So you say, "Hey Judas," and Jude looks up, or you say, "Hey Jude," and Judas looks up. What a mess, it was crazy.

42 One of these guys, Judas Iscariot, I liked him at first, he knew what was what. But he came to a bad end, Judas did, I'll get to that later. I had nothing to do with it, don't believe what the fake scribes say.

43 He had twelve apostles now, but he had his favorites. They were Peter, John, and James, he was always taking them aside, and the other nine didn't like it, and neither did I. One day he took them up this mountain, and I followed, but I stayed out of sight.

44 So they're on the mountain, and all of a sudden, it was freaky, Jesus's face just lit up like the sun. And his robe, it was usually dirty, but now it was this pure white, and it was shining. How he did that, I'll never know. Probably something to do with mirrors, or brimstone, who knows.

45 Then these two old guys showed up, I don't know from where. They just seemed to appear out of nowhere, like some kind of trick using mirrors or something, that's what it looked like. They were two raggedy looking dudes, one of them looked like John the Batshit, only older, but it couldn't have been him, he was dead.

46 Then a bright white cloud came down, and I heard a voice come out of the sky, like the one on the Jordan River, and it said, ***"This is my beloved son, in whom I am well pleased."*** Just what it said back on the Jordan. Peter and John and James, they fell down on the ground, and the two old guys slipped away somehow, they just disappeared into thin air.

47 I wasn't that close, I couldn't tell exactly what happened, but I figured they were practicing a new trick or something. You have to keep the act fresh, you have to come up with new material. As they came back down the mountain, I hid behind a bush, and I heard Jesus say, **Tell the vision to no man, until the Son of man be risen again from the dead.**

48 They were up to something, alright. What did he mean, "risen again from the dead?" But I'll get to that later, too.

49 So anyway, now all twelve of them go with Jesus to Cana, this little shithole town in Galilee. There was a wedding, and Jesus's mother, Mary, the "virgin"—you remember her, the Vermin Mary—well, she was there.

50 I told you about these Jews and their mothers. You've never seen anything like it, they're going after each other all the time. First thing Mary does, she starts whining to Jesus that there's no wine. A wedding with no wine, I mean, what were they thinking? It was a disaster, a total disgrace.

51 Jesus says to his mother, **Woman, what have I to do with you? My hour has not yet come.** I figure, he's not ready to start drinking, okay? But this Mary, she's not giving in. She tells the servants, do whatever my kid tells you to do, and she gives Jesus this look, like, you better get some wine here, buddy.

52 There were these six huge waterpots sitting there. The Jews use these waterpots for bathing, they bathe all the time, like they're being baptized over

and over. That guilt thing, it's crazy. Obsessed with being clean, these Jews, like you can wash away sins. They'll never forget John the Batshit, trust me on that.

53 So Jesus, he tells the servants, **Fill the waterpots with water.** They fill the waterpots, and Jesus tells them, **Draw out the water now, and bear it to the governor of the feast.** The governor, he takes a sip, and allakazam! It's not water at all, it's wine!

54 Another setup, and what a trick! Water turned into wine, who wouldn't love *that*? What better way to get people to follow you—you tell them, "Drinks are on me!"

55 So I tell Jesus, I say, "Look, this is all great, I mean, really terrific. But you have to monetize the act, you have to make money, see? Why not bottle the wine, and put a label on it: 'Delicious Miracle Kosher Wine, Anytime. From the Vineyards of Jesus of Nazareth, Bottled by the Apostles and Blessed by the God of the Jews.'"

56 What an idea! But what does he do? You guessed it, he gives me that sad smile of his, shakes his head a little, and walks off. I mean, the guy was a great magician, the best, but he had no business sense.

57 I figured they were making their money here and there, because nobody works for free, right? They must have been taking a few shekels for a healing, selling some of those fish to their fans, maybe a catering fee for the wedding, who knows. But that's all small change.

58 Monetize it, I say! What good is branding if you don't monetize? At my baths, we sell soaps, we have a towel service, we have massage girls. At my casinos, we sell wine, we serve food, we have massage girls. At my inns, we do it all—the wine, the food, the soaps, the towels, the massage girls. Money, money, money! That's what it's all about.

59 But Jesus, he must have had something else in mind. It wasn't selling tickets, he wouldn't sell a single one. I tried, believe me I tried, to get him to sell tickets. But he wouldn't do it, he wouldn't sell tickets.

60 Hell, I never even knew when his next trick would come—I mean, his next miracle—or his next faith healing, or his next sermon, or the next baptism and wet tunic contest. How do you sell tickets when people don't know when the next show will be? You have to brand, you have to monetize, but for goodness' sake, you have to promote!

61 They were going to make money somehow, that was for sure. Maybe it was going to be tithing, where you get these peasants and zealots, these rubes, to give you ten percent of everything they make. That's what the Jews were doing already, collecting ten percent, like a tax. Maybe they were out to muscle into the tithing racket. Now that would be monetizing, bigly.

62 Or maybe they were going to pass around a plate at the sermons, take up a collection. That's easier than selling tickets. Or maybe they were going to put the squeeze on the locals for some protection, you know, pay up and you'll get a little miracle, don't pay up and who knows what might happen. Or maybe it was a little bit of each—some tithing, some collections, some protection.

63 Well, he had to do *something* with this wine. So I think about it, and I come up with another idea. You take this wine he makes out of water, and you put it into old bottles, and you sell it as aged wine. You know, "A dry red masterpiece from the reign of Julius Caesar," or, "A tantalizing white from the year of the 175th Olympiad."

64 You jack up the price five, maybe ten times, and you make a fortune. It was foolproof!

65 Now remember, I've offered him a million sesterces, then ten million, and I'm following him around and offering up the best swag I have—new shoes, silk robes, the best food, massage girls—but nothing's working. So, new wine in old bottles! A fortune, I'm telling you. And I pitch it hard, I mean, really hard.

66 What does he do? Do I even have to tell you? Yup, he smiles that sad smile of his, he shakes his head, and he says, **No one puts new wine in old bottles, or else the new wine bursts the bottles, and the wine is spilled, and the bottles will be marred: but new wine must be put into new bottles, and**

both are preserved. Like I said, no business sense at all, at least not as far as I could tell.

67 He was getting bigger and bigger all the time. The crowds just loved him, people fell all over each other to be near him.

68 But he did seem to have an idea or two, and maybe one of them was franchising. See, he had these twelve apostles now, and some of them were doing their own magic shows. And they were drawing crowds, too, just for being his assistants.

69 Maybe he knew what to do with them, and maybe he didn't. I told him, send them all out on the road—that's twelve extra shows, blanketing the whole empire, maybe even beyond. A real cash cow, it would've made millions, let me tell you.

70 Like I said, I wasn't giving up. There was money to be made, and by Jupiter, Donald of Gaul was going to get in on it.

6 I have to give Jesus credit, he took my advice again. He sent these apostles running all over the eastern Mediterranean, and they were all baptizing and healing and doing whatever little magic tricks they could. They were finally getting this traveling preacher franchise thing up and running, everybody was talking about them, they were getting big, really big.

2 Jesus, he was still the main act. He kept a couple apostles around him and sent the rest out on the B-list circuit. You know, the small towns and back-waters, you have to make a buck wherever you can. He sent them out in pairs, which, if you ask me, is just cutting your profits in half.

3 I was there when they had their first sales meeting, it was beautiful. Finally, some organization! So at this sales meeting, he gives them a little pep talk, and he tells them their target market is the Jews.

4 He says, **Go not into the way of the Gentiles, and into any city of the Samaritans enter not: but go rather to the lost sheep of the house of Israel. And as you go, preach, saying, The kingdom of heaven is at hand.**

5 I'm thinking, now we're getting somewhere! Sales territories and a target market, that's how you monetize. I didn't know what he meant about the "kingdom of heaven" yet, but it was crazy, you'll see.

6 Then he lays out the schtick, he says, **Heal the sick, cleanse the lepers, raise the dead, cast out devils; freely you have received, freely you shall give.**

7 Quite a list of magic tricks! It was terrific, really terrific. But free? What the hell was that all about? Maybe I wasn't getting through to him at all, you can't give it away for free. You have to hustle, you have to make money. The point is, you can't be *too* greedy, there's no such thing. Greed is good, that's what I always say.

8 But he did one thing right, he didn't give them any expense accounts at all, and he told them to travel light. Control your expenses, that's how to maximize profits.

9 He says, **Take nothing for your journey, neither staves, nor scrip, neither bread, nor money; for the workman is worthy of his meat; neither have two coats apiece, nor shoes. And into whatever city or town you enter, enquire who in it is worthy; and whatever house you enter into, remain there till you depart.**

10 Pretty tough, bumming around for food and crashing in people's houses like that. I didn't like that part, though, not one bit. What would happen to my inn and tavern business if you could just get a bed and a breakfast anywhere, out of thin air like that? But it would keep expenses low, so maybe Jesus had some business sense after all.

11 I still figured I could sign him up, so I kept my people on him with the offers and the swag. And I followed him wherever I could, but he was on the road now, schlepping all over Judea and Galilee, building that brand and working the Son of God angle like nobody's business.

12 He was really into the faith healer thing, it was amazing. Anyone can pretend to heal a leper or make a blind man see, but it takes a real showman to turn it into an act—you know, to really sell it. Boy was he good at it, and I figure he taught the apostles to do it right, just like his dad Gabriel probably taught him.

13 But he took it even farther, pretending to cast devils out of people. I guess that's an easy trick, too. All you need is someone to act like they're crazy, and you smack them on the forehead and say some magic words. Then they roll their eyes in the back of their head and speak some nonsense. Presto, no more demon!

14 As if that wasn't enough, this thing about raising the dead was something else. Get some shill to pretend he's dead, stick him in a tomb, then allakazam, allakazoo, out he pops, like he's fresh as a daisy again. They were doing it all over the place, at least that's what people were telling me. I hadn't seen it myself, at least not yet. (It didn't turn out well, trust me.)

15 All this casting out devils, raising the dead, being the son of God, maybe it was getting to be too much. He was pissing off the Pharisees and the priests. The Pharisees and the priests in the Temple, they were the top dogs among the Jews. They ran the show in Jerusalem, and they didn't like anything new—they had the power, they got the tithes, why would they want to change things?

16 Jesus had guts, that's for sure. He wasn't afraid of the authorities, not the Pharisees, not the priests, not even the Romans. And they were all keeping an eye on him by now, that much I knew. I knew people in high places in Jerusalem, I always schmooze with the higher-ups, and they wanted to shut him down.

17 But he was sharp, he was really working the circuit by now. He didn't slow down for the Sabbath, either. The Jews, they're not supposed to work on the Sabbath day, like I said before. They're supposed to give one day a week to their God, this NoWay.

18 The Sabbath, really? Why cut your profits by a seventh just for a bunch of goody two shoes like these Pharisees? Who does that? If I want some fried

chicken, I don't care what day of the week it is. I'm not going to say it's nuts, but if you want to give away a seventh of your profits, go ahead, even if it's nuts.

19 Anyway, he was stepping on the toes of some very powerful people. After all I did to keep Herod Antipasto off his ass, and Tiberius Caesar, too, he goes around acting like that. Big league mistake, I have to tell you, big league.

20 So one day he's on the Sea of Galilee again, at another backwater town called Bethsaida. I was there, it was awful, a real shithole. He's called all his apostles there for a corporate meeting, probably to do some strategizing. Branding, monetizing, promoting—it's not kid's stuff, okay?

21 And he's preaching to a big crowd, a really big crowd, almost as big as one of mine. (I've had bigger rallies, way bigger, but the fake scribes won't admit it.) There were so many people following him now that he could hardly give a decent sermon.

22 He can barely do a simple magic trick without the people swarming all over him. And he gets fed up, so he stops in the middle of the act, and he goes up this mountain with his apostles, and they take a break. Maybe they have a business meeting, who knows? I'm just guessing, because I didn't go up there with them, I stayed behind.

23 Then this crowd, it's getting restless, see? They want a show, it's getting late, and they're getting hungry. So the apostles, they tell Jesus to make the people scram, there's way too many of them to feed. But no, Jesus, he has another idea.

24 He says, **They need not depart; give them something to eat. How many loaves have you? Go and see.**

25 They tell him, "We have here but five loaves and two fishes." Five loaves of bread and two fishes. Great Neptune, I can eat two fishes myself, and five loaves of bread? That's barely enough to feed the thirteen of them fish sandwiches, am I right?

26 So there's five loaves of bread and two fishes. Jesus, he says, **Bring them here to me.** The apostles, they're wondering what the hell he's doing, but I

figured it out right away—he was setting up another magic trick. He looks at the audience, and he says, **Make them sit down by fifties in a company.**

27 There were hundreds of men there, maybe thousands, plus a whole mess of women and children. The apostles, they line these people up like cattle, in groups of fifty, or maybe a hundred. Who knows, it's not easy to count that many people.

28 Then Jesus, he holds these two fishes and these five loaves of bread up to the sky, and he says some hocus pocus, and he starts to break them into pieces and give them to the apostles. I'll be damned if I know how he did it, but you should've seen it. They divvied up the grub, and spread it to the crowd, and everyone, thousands of them, ate like it was the Feast of Fornicalia!

29 I had some myself, it wasn't the best, not by my standards. But for these hillbillies, it was top notch, and everyone ate their fill. Now everyone's sitting around fat and happy, and Jesus says, **Gather up the fragments that remain, that nothing be lost.** Good for him, you have to control waste, that's how you maximize profits.

30 Do you believe it, there were twelve baskets of fish and bread left over! Holy Ceres, how the hell did he pull *that* off? It was fabulous, let me tell you.

31 So I go and grab Jesus, and I tell him, "Jesus Christ!" (He loved to be called that, who wouldn't?) I say, "Jesus Christ, you've got a gold mine here! A string of restaurants, the Jesus Joint, the Christ Café, whatever you want to call them. All-you-can-eat fish and chips, two or three quadrans a plate. Dine in, carry out, maybe some delivery. Think of the profit margins! You're talking major denaro!"

32 It was my best idea yet, a real winner. It couldn't miss. Throw in the wine he made out of water, and you're talking about a fortune.

33 But what does Jesus do? Yup, he smiles that sad smile of his, shakes his head, and off he walks. Again.

34 But he's not done with the magic, not by a long shot. He gets his apostles together, and he sends them across the Sea of Galilee in a boat, towards

another hillbilly backwater on the other side called Capernaum. Then he tells the crowd to go on home, and he goes back up the mountain.

35 Well, there were plenty of people who stayed, and so did I. And before you know it, a storm blew up, a really strong one. The waves, they were like, three, maybe four feet high. Those apostles, there they were, right in the middle of the Sea of Galilee, rowing like their lives depended on it, and the sail was flapping like crazy.

36 Then here comes Jesus, walking right across the water, just like he was on dry land. What a trick! It was amazing, just amazing! By Veritas, he was walking on water, right in front of our eyes! The people, they went crazy, pointing their fingers and oohing and aahing. And the apostles, they started screaming like a bunch of babies afraid to take a bath. Losers, all twelve of them, no better than women.

37 Jesus, he says, **Be of good cheer, it is I; be not afraid.** The fools, they were assistants to the world's greatest magician, they should've known a good trick when they saw one. Aint Peter, maybe he was less of a loser than the others, or maybe he was in on the trick. He sees Jesus walking on the water, and he says, "Lord, if it be thou, bid me to come to you on the water."

38 So Jesus says, **Come.** And Peter, he steps out of the boat, and he takes a few steps towards Jesus, and he's walking on water himself. But he hasn't learned the trick quite yet, and he starts to sink, and Jesus grabs him and helps him back into the boat.

39 Jesus says to Aint Peter, **O you of little faith, why did you doubt?** I figured he was just razzing Aint Peter a little. You know, you have to keep your people in line sometimes, at least that's how I do it with my people. A little bit of razzing, it keeps them on their toes.

40 So they row the rest of the way to Capernaum. The crowd on the Bethsaida side of the sea all start to scramble, they jump into any boat they can find and make for Capernaum, too. The people in Capernaum, they've all heard the stories by now, and they practically swamp Jesus's boat trying to get a piece of him.

41 All I can think about is that walking on water trick. Probably put cork in his sandals and tied a rope to the boat, or something like that. Not a bad idea, I could sell that at all my resort inns around the Mediterranean. "Fun for the whole family," something like that. Kids would be falling all over each other to get their parents to take them, it couldn't miss.

42 So I track down Jesus one more time, and there he is, sitting down on the seashore with a bunch of little kids, it was, like, twenty or thirty filthy little brats. I say, "Jesus Christ, that walking on water trick was fantastic! Tell me how you do it, and I'll cut you in for forty percent—no, make it fifty. You don't have to do a thing, just let me in on the secret."

43 Do I even have to tell you what he did? Jesus, he smiles that sad smile, he shakes his head, and he starts to walk away. But no, I'm not done yet. The man just won't listen to reason.

44 So I say, "Jesus Effing Christ, listen!" (He didn't like to be called that so much.) "You can make all the money you'll ever need right here on the seashore, with nothing but seawater. All-you-can-eat seafood. Water into wine. Walking on water concessions. Seawater, for Pete's sake, it's nothing but seawater. It's free, it's everywhere! Cash in, man, cash in! Get your reward! You could have a kingdom for a little seawater!"

45 He turns back to me, and in that meek little voice of his, with that sweet little smile still on his lips, he says, **The kingdom of heaven is like a net that was cast into the sea, and gathered every kind of fish; which, when it was full, they drew to shore, and sat down, and gathered the good fish into vessels, but cast the bad fish away.**

46 Then he pauses, like he's expecting me to say something. But I don't know what to say, I just shrug my shoulders. And he looks around at all those kids, and he says, **If you say, 'Look, the Kingdom is in the sea!' then the fish will be there before you are. Go to the sea, then, and cast a hook, and take up the first fish that comes up, and when you have opened his mouth, you shall find a piece of money: take that, and give it to Caesar for me and you.**

47 Finally, he was ready to talk money, but he wasn't making any sense. Maybe he was drunk, I don't know, but what kind of mumbo jumbo was he talking? What the hell was this "kingdom of heaven" crap? So I tell those kids to beat it, they're getting on my nerves, and we adults have business to discuss, and boy do they scram! Then he says,

48 **Suffer the little children to come to me, and forbid them not: for of such is the kingdom of heaven. Whoever shall give one of these little ones a cup of cold water to drink only in the name of a disciple, truly I say to you, he shall in no way lose his reward.**

49 **But whoever shall offend one of these little children who believe in me, it were better for him that a millstone was hung about his neck, and he was drowned in the depth of the sea.**

50 I figured, maybe some fake scribes had told him I wasn't nice to children. Well what if I'm not? What the hell am I, a nursemaid? Some kid can't get cold water to drink, what's that got to do with me? Some slave or refugee kid gets put in a pen, hey, so what? Some kid has the palsy, I don't care if it's my own nephew's baby, it's not my problem.

51 So I'm just about to lose it. I get ready to really lay into him, okay? And boy, you don't want to be around when I tell someone off, believe me. But he hangs his head for a second, then he looks at the sky, like he's looking for something. An angel, maybe, or a dove, who the hell knows. Then he says,

52 **Get behind me, Donald; for you savor not the things that be of God, but the things that be of men. For what shall it profit a man, if he shall gain the whole world, and lose his own soul? Or what shall a man give in exchange for his soul?**

53 I was just about to give him an answer. I had an accountant with me that day, along with this secretary from Sodom—you should've seen her, she was incredible, she wrote down everything we said that day. So I asked the accountant what a soul was worth, and he sort of scratched his head and started counting on his fingers.

54 Venus and Visucius, I was ready to give him an answer, alright, but he just shook his head and walked away. *Again.* Maybe I should have given up right then. Maybe there was no way to get through to this guy.

55 But like I said, when I want something, I get it. And damned if I was going to give up on this Jesus. He was the best performer I'd ever seen, and he was going to perform for me, Donald of Gaul, one way or another.

56 He was holding out for more money, that's what I figured. I may not know how much a soul is worth, but I damn well know how much a ticket to the best magic show in the empire is worth!

57 And if I had to pay this guy top denarius, so be it.

7 The next day, Jesus climbs this little mountain, and people are following him like sheep. There's thousands of them, more than I've ever seen. The apostles are there doing some crowd control.

2 I figured this was going to be one helluva show. After the water into wine and the loaves and the fishes and the walking on water, I figured he was ready for a grand finale, something big, something really, really big.

3 I had my secretary there, the one from Sodom, she wrote down every word he said that day. It was one helluva sermon, alright, he had the crowd in the palm of his hand. But what a letdown! There was no healing, no demon casting, no raising the dead, no doves, no voices, not a single magic trick.

4 He just talked. And talked and talked and talked. A little sermon on a mount, who the hell is going to remember that? And the things he said, they made no sense at all.

5 What a letdown! The public is fickle, one day you're in, the next day you're out. Just ask any gladiator, just ask any dancing girl. Hell, just ask any senator or emperor—if you don't give the people what they want, they'll turn on you just like that.

6 So that night, I arrange a sit down, a real face-to-face, right there on that little mountain. You might say, a summit, just me and Jesus, and my secretary, of course. I needed her there to remind him of the crazy things he'd said. Right at the beginning of this sermon, he'd said, **Blessed are the meek: for they shall inherit the earth.**

7 Now look, this world, it's tough, see? You have to be tough, you have to give as good as you take. Jesus, he was such a pushover, I just wanted to toughen him up. So I say to him, I say, "Jesus, what's this shit about the meek inheriting the earth? That's crazy. The meek, they get run over. Nice guys finish last, everyone knows that."

8 It's true, right? So I tell him, I say, "When someone attacks me, I always attack back, except ten times harder. Every time, no matter what. A senator, a general, a widow, a little girl in pigtails—it doesn't matter who, you hit back, and you hit back hard."

9 Jesus, he shakes his head—I was getting really, really annoyed with that—and he repeats what he said in the sermon again. He says, **Agree with your adversary quickly, while you are in the way with him. Whoever shall smite you on your right cheek, turn to him the other cheek also.**

10 I'm like, yeah, right! Turn the other cheek. I say, "Anybody who hits me, I'm going to hit ten, maybe twenty times harder," that's what I tell him. He's still repeating things from that sermon, so he says,

11 **Judge not, that you be not judged. For with what judgment you judge, you shall be judged: and with what measure you mete, it shall be measured to you again. And why behold you the mote that is in your brother's eye, but consider not the beam that is in your own eye? For if you forgive men their trespasses, your heavenly Father will also forgive you: but if you forgive not men their trespasses, neither will your Father forgive your trespasses.**

12 Well, I knew all about his Son of God schtick, but this was me, Donald of Gaul, he was talking to. My father was no slouch, he was one tough son of a bitch. He taught me to fight like hell for anything I want—"You're a killer,

you're a king," he'd say—and if people get in the way, that's their problem, you just crush them.

13 Forgive, my ass. You don't forgive, and you don't forget. When someone gets in your way, you crush them, completely, and whatever someone does to you, no matter how small, you get revenge. Revenge, that's for winners. Forgiveness, that's for losers, it's weak, very weak.

14 So I say, "When people go against you, you have to go after those people, hard, because other people will see you doing it, and they'll stay out of your way from then on. I always get even, that's what I do, and then some. You can't be weak, you have to take it right to them! They're the enemy, got it?"

15 Jesus, he wrinkles his brow a little, and he says what he said the day before: **You have heard that it has been said, You shall love your neighbor, and hate your enemy. But I say to you, love your enemies, bless them that curse you, do good to them that hate you, and pray for them that despitefully use you, and persecute you.**

16 **That you may be the child of your Father which is in heaven: for he makes his sun to rise on the evil and on the good, and sends rain on the just and the unjust. Be you therefore perfect, even as your Father which is in heaven is perfect.**

17 Perfect? If anyone's perfect, it's me, but that's because I'm strong, not because I'm weak. Jesus tried to tell me that hate and rancor should be removed from our hearts. I don't think so. Enemies are enemies, and of course, I hate those people. Let's all hate those people, our enemies, because maybe hate is what we need if we're going to get something done.

18 And who the hell am I going to pray for? Take care of number one, that's what I say. Nobody prays for me, I don't believe it, nobody follows that crap, everybody's out for number one. I don't like people who use their faith to justify what they know is wrong, I don't like people who say "I pray for you" when you know that is not so. It's all bullshit.

19 So Jesus, he starts to say something about John the Batshit, but I'm not in the mood to talk about that loser. Ask for forgiveness, wash away sins, repent,

blah blah blah. So I say, "I don't like to have to ask for forgiveness. Why do I have to repent, why do I have to ask for forgiveness if I'm not making mistakes?"

20 Then he brings up the Ten Commandments—these rules, or laws, that Moses supposedly got straight from Yahweh. I mean, NoWay. He says, **Whoever shall break one of these least commandments, he shall be called the least in the kingdom of heaven: but whoever shall do and teach them, the same shall be called great in the kingdom of heaven.**

21 **For I say to you, that except your righteousness shall exceed the righteousness of the scribes and Pharisees, you shall in no case enter into the kingdom of heaven.**

22 Holy crap, he's back into this "kingdom of heaven" thing. How the hell do you argue with that? And these commandments, who the hell has the right to command *me*? I'm Donald of Gaul, dammit! I had a kingdom already, probably six, maybe eight billion sesterces' worth.

23 But I don't want to piss him off, so I stick it to the fake scribes and Pharisees. I say, "Hey, I'm not like the fake scribes, they're very dishonest people, okay? And those Pharisees, what a bunch of goody two shoes!"

24 Then I start laying it on thick, telling him how I haven't killed anyone, how I don't commit adultery, how I don't steal. That's what the ten commandments are all about. I know, because I had one of my secretaries look them up in the Library of Alexandria.

25 What a worthless place that is, the Library of Alexandria, just a bunch of scrolls and maps and crap. Libraries are for losers, they're pathetic. Julius Caesar should have burned that place all the way to the ground when he had the chance. No libraries for me, I don't need a damn library, believe me.

26 Anyway, I go on, I tell him how much I pray, and how much I give to the poor, and how I fast. That was all bullshit, of course. But like I said, you tell people what they want to hear. That's how you get what you want—you tell them what they want to hear, you make it simple, you repeat it over and over again.

27 But Jesus, he looks me in the eye, and in a not-so-meek voice, he says, **Beware of the scribes, which love to go in long clothing, and love salutations in the marketplace, and the chief seats in the synagogues, and the uppermost rooms in feasts: Which devour widow's houses, and for a pretence make long prayers: these shall receive greater damnation.**

28 Well, I have to admit, I shuddered a little at that. He had his apostles keeping an eye on me, I was sure of it. He was no fool, that Jesus! But you don't spy on me, Donald of Gaul. Me, you don't spy on.

29 Yeah, maybe I had been making a big show in Jerusalem, at the marketplace, and the synagogues, and the feasts. And yeah, maybe I did make some long prayers. Why not? I was working a deal, I was making connections. So what if I didn't believe any of that mumbo jumbo?

30 But how did he know about the widow, I forget her name, how did he know about that old bat's house? Yeah, maybe I did try to get her evicted from her house, but what the hell? I needed that space to park chariots for one of my biggest casinos! And what was this "damnation" crap? Who was he to be damning me?

31 So he starts going on and on and on, like, **Take heed that you do not your alms before men, to be seen of them: when you do alms, do not sound a trumpet before you, as the hypocrites do in the synagogues and in the streets, that they may have glory of men. Truly I say to you, they have their reward.**

32 **But when you do alms, let not your left hand know what your right hand does: That your alms may be in secret: and your Father which sees in secret himself shall reward you openly.**

33 "No, no, no," I tell him, "You've got it all wrong! Holy smokes! See, here's what you do—you start a little charity, and you get a bunch of money from people who want to kiss up to you, then you go out and spread it around in a big giveaway right there in front of everybody, with bells and whistles and dancing girls.

34 "Give some alms to a few lepers, give some alms to a few beggars, what the hell, just throw handfuls at the peasants and let them scramble for it. Make a big show of it, so you get all the credit. And the best part is, you don't even have to use your own money."

35 He sort of smiles and looks at the ground, shaking his head like he always did. Then he says, **When you pray, you shall not be as the hypocrites are: for they love to pray standing in the synagogues and in the corners of the streets, that they may be seen of men. Truly I say to you, they have their reward.**

36 **But you, when you pray, enter into your closet, and when you have shut your door, pray to your Father, which is in secret: and your Father which sees in secret shall reward you openly.**

37 I just about bust a gut at that one. "Are you kidding me?" I say. "Look, here's what you do—you get a holy book, a Torah or whatever, and you make it a big one. I have a huge one, I tell everyone it was my mother's, people eat that up. And I hold it up high, right there in the temple, and I pray as loud as I can. Make a big show of it, don't you see?"

38 Jesus, he's not done yet, oh no. He says, **Moreover, when you fast, be not, as the hypocrites, of a sad countenance: for they disfigure their faces, that they may appear to men to fast. Truly I say to you, they have their reward.**

39 **But you, when you fast, anoint your head, and wash your face; that you appear not to men to fast, but to your Father which is in secret: and your Father, which sees in secret, shall reward you openly.**

40 Well, how do you argue with anything that damn crazy? Forty days and forty nights he spent fasting in the desert, and for what? To tell his father? At least get some good publicity out of it, that's what I would have done. And why did he keep talking about his father, anyway? What did Gabriel have to do with anything?

41 So I figure, I'll take another tack. I say, "Jesus Christ, look at me. I'm worth eight, maybe ten billion sesterces. Who has God rewarded more than

me? I'm the richest man in the empire, except the emperor, Praise Be to Caesar. Just look at my rewards, I…"

42 Just then, it hit me—maybe he wasn't so dense after all. Maybe it was all about the payoff, the reward: "Your father shall *reward* you." Maybe he was offering the suckers something that I hadn't heard about. That's Marketing 101, everyone wants to know, what's in it for *me*?

43 Yeah, maybe Jesus was a step ahead of me. Maybe he figured that the way to get the most out of people with this traveling preacher flimflam is to promise them the moon. Tell them, if you follow me, and pray to this God of mine, and maybe, give me ten percent of everything you have, well, God will grant your every wish. He'll make you rich, richer than you ever imagined.

44 Riches! *That's* what you sell these rubes—only you use a bigger word, like that scriptwriter of Jesus's would, something like "prosperity." The more you give *me*, the more prosperity God'll give *you*. And all the magic and healing and demon casting and raising of the dead, all the miracles you can scrounge up, you and your apostles, that's just window dressing to get people to pony up.

45 Maybe he was right, Jesus was, you don't need to sell tickets. That's just chump change. Make them think you're the Son of God, then take every quadrans and dupondius and denarius you can get. Take them for ten percent of everything they've got. That's what the Jew priests do, why not Jesus, too?

46 Finally, I had this guy figured out. He was holding out for the big score, the long con. So I lay it all out, I tell him I know what he's up to. It's all about the tithing. I tell him, "I get it, you're just waiting for the big payoff down the road, the tithes. That's what you're up to, I knew it was something."

47 For a second there, I thought I had him. But no, what does he do? There comes that little smile, and that meek little voice, and he says:

48 **Lay not up for yourself treasures on earth, where moth and rust do corrupt, and where thieves break through and steal: But lay up for yourself treasures in heaven, where neither moth nor rust do corrupt, and where thieves do not break through nor steal: For where your treasure is, there will your heart also be.**

49 Talk about nuts! Everyone wants some treasure, am I right? All the best stories are about some treasure buried in the desert or on an island somewhere. Diamonds, rubies, silver, gold—who doesn't want that? And what was this heaven crap? I still didn't get it.

50 So I tell him, I say, "Jesus, you've got it all wrong! Here's what you do—you get a vault, see? A big one. And you make it climate controlled, and you have an exterminator. Bing bang bong, no rust! No moths! And you get a good centurion, I mean, a really good centurion, and you hire some muscle, see? You pay them well, and bim boom bam, no thieves!" A perfect plan, if I do say so myself.

51 He didn't seem impressed. He just looked at the ground and said, **If you will be perfect, go and sell all that you have, and give it to the poor, and you shall have treasure in heaven: and come and follow me.**

52 **Truly I say to you, That a rich man shall hardly enter into the kingdom of heaven. It is easier for a camel to go through the eye of a needle, than for a rich man to enter into the kingdom of God. You cannot serve both God and money.**

53 Yeah, right, sell *everything I have* and give it to the poor. Who did he think he was dealing with? He was trying to take my whole fortune, every denarius, for himself and his crooked daddy, Gabriel! So maybe that was the scam… don't just sell tickets, or take ten percent, but take it all, the whole schmear.

54 So I ask him, I say, "Okay, let's just say that I sell all my real estate. What then? What's in it for *me?*"

55 And he says, real slow and sure, he says, **Every one that has forsaken houses, or lands, for my name's sake, shall receive back a hundred times, and shall inherit everlasting life.**

56 Finally, he lays it on the line. Not a bad pitch, I have to admit. Give me everything you have, and you'll get it back times a hundred. *Times a hundred!* Plus—and every ad man knows you have to say, "But there's *more!*"—plus, you'll live forever.

57 Live forever! So *that's* what he meant about "the kingdom of heaven." You'll never die—you'll just go to heaven and live forever with this God, this Yahweh. The "father" he kept talking about wasn't Crooked Gabriel, it was Yahweh. And the kingdom of heaven was, literally, heaven!

58 This whole time he'd been setting me up, just waiting for the right moment to go in for the kill. Never try to close the deal until the time is ripe, that's what I always say, that's the art of the deal.

59 Those apostles, they must've been running all over the empire doing the same thing, softening up marks and then hitting them with that pitch. Sell everything you have, and Yahweh will give you back that much times a hundred, plus a condo in paradise, this "kingdom of heaven," after you die.

60 Jupiter only knows how much they'd already collected. Enough to make Crooked Gabriel filthy rich, I was sure of that.

61 Well, that was the end of it. Here was Jesus, trying to con me, Donald of Gaul, out of everything I own. Don the Con, the greatest of them all! I can con my way into anything, and I do mean, *anything*. Who the hell did he think he was talking to?

62 Yahweh? I said to myself, No Way! No way in hell.

63 Every good salesman knows, once you give your pitch, you shut up. The next person who talks, loses. This Gabriel, he taught Jesus well, because Jesus, he doesn't say a word. He just looks at me with those big brown eyes and that sad smile of his.

64 Well, I wasn't playing his game, not today. So I say, "Are you talking to *me*? Donald of Gaul? Hell no, I'm not selling a damn thing, not for you or anybody else. Do you think I was born yesterday? Jesus Effing Christ!" (He really didn't like to be called that, but I was hot, let me tell you, really hot.) "Let me tell *you* something…"

65 But this guy, this Jesus, he just looks at the sky, shakes his head, and turns his back on me—on me, Donald of Gaul—and walks away.

66 Again. But maybe, for the last time.

8 So now I say to myself, I say, "Donald, this thing, it's coming to a head. You have to make your move. The gig is up, they're not fooling The Donald. They're working the travelling preacher racket to the hilt, the cash is flowing, the big payoff could be just around the corner. You have to get in on it. Now."

2 And here's what I know: First, there's this get rich quick scheme. Give us all you got, and this God here, Yahweh, he's going to make you rich—he'll get you back everything you had times a hundred. Not a bad return on your investment. Greed, that's a mighty powerful tool.

3 Second, you're going to live forever, you're never going to die. Fear of death, that's what they're counting on. Fear, that's a powerful tool, even more powerful than greed.

4 And third, where are you going to live? In paradise, that's where! In this kingdom of heaven, wherever that is. You die, then *zip!* Off you go, and some angel gives you the keys. A real estate development in the clouds. What a concept!

5 And if you don't pay up, well, who knows what might happen. But I'll get to that later, it was a protection racket like you've never seen, believe me.

6 It was the greatest scam ever—the Ultimate Con. And how do you close the deal? With magic! You make voices come out of the sky, you do some hocus pocus with the clouds, you make a dove land on your shoulder, you turn water into wine, you turn a few fish into an all-you-can-eat buffet, you cure some diseases, you cast out some demons, you walk on water—I mean, come on, it was genius!

7 And last of all, what was maybe the key to the whole thing—you bring some shills back from the dead. Six feet under, pushing up daisies, kaput—then badda bing, a little alakazam, and these shills, they're right back on their feet in the Land of the Living.

8 Back from the dead. If you can make them believe *that*, you've got them in the palm of your hand. They'll believe in living forever, alright, they'll think they've seen it with their own two eyes.

9 I figured, there must be millions of suckers out there who'd fall for this hustle. And what's your average peasant worth, a thousand measly sesterces? A thousand marks, at a thousand sesterces apiece, that's, like, almost a million sesterces, right? And a million marks, at a few thousand sesterces apiece, that's, like, almost a billion! And with one rich patsy, like me, you could take in, like, billions!

10 So I go to my top accountant in Rome—he's a Jew, like I said, that's who you want counting your money. I lay out the whole scam, and I ask him, I say, "Finkelstein, high pathetically speaking, how much could this grift be worth?"

11 And he says, "Donald, a million marks at a thousand sesterces, that's a billion sesterces. Ten million marks at ten thousand sesterces, that's a hundred billion sesterces."

12 Bingo! I almost had a cow! A hundred billion, and that's *on top* of what we'd be making at my properties! And here I was, worth ten, maybe twelve billion sesterces. I could double it, triple it, maybe more, the sky was the limit.

13 I knew one more thing, and it was key: the boss wasn't Jesus. No, hell no, the boss was his father, Crooked Gabriel. I had to see *him*, and I had to do it fast. You have to go to the top, that's how you get things done.

14 So then I go to my lawyers, Kohn and Kohen—Jews, of course, and boy, these guys were the best. Kohn was older than me, he was my mentor, he taught me everything I know. How to pay off praetors, put the squeeze on Senators, kiss up to consuls, even get the ear of the emperor, he could do it all.

15 Kohen was my hatchet man, I used him to do all the dirty work. There was nothing he wouldn't do for me—pay off mistresses, fiddle with taxes, run insurance scams, do collections, knock some heads, you name it.

16 Kohn and Kohen, they write up a contract for Jesus, worth—get this—a hundred million sesterces. *A hundred million!* More scratch than this guy's ever seen or even thought of.

17 Back I go to Judea, that shithole, and let me tell you, I was getting tired of it. In Rome I had everything—the best rooms, the best food, the best baths,

the best girls, all I had to do was snap my fingers. In Judea, you should have seen how the people lived. Even the best inns were like living in a dog kennel, it was disgusting, totally disgusting.

18 Well, by now Jesus was on the run from the Romans and the priests and the Pharisees. I knew it would happen, he pissed off the wrong people, and these people, you really don't want to piss them off. But I had my people watching him.

19 I also had a guy in deep, really deep, maybe you can guess who. And he got word to me to come back to Bethabara, on the Jordan River. Bethabara, that's where I first found John the Batshit, that's where I saw John baptize Jesus at the wet tunic contest. That's where this whole mess got started. And what a mess, it was turning into a total disaster.

20 We get there, and we ask around, and everyone clams up. Everyone there, they remembered John the Batshit, and they knew he was dead, and they remembered Jesus, but they wouldn't say a word about where he was. They knew he was on the lam, and most of them thought he was this savior of theirs, so they wouldn't spill the beans, they wouldn't rat him out.

21 We finally get some information from a centurion working for Herod Antipasto. Turns out, Jesus had just left for Bethany, another shithole, it was a suburb of Jerusalem. (*Beth*abara, *Beth*lehem, *Beth*saida, *Beth*any, *Beth*-Aram— what the hell? Who was this Beth chick? I don't know, but she sure got around, I can tell you that.)

22 Like I said, Jesus was on the run from the top bosses of the Jews, and their temple was in Jerusalem. He was on the run from the Romans, who were everywhere, but the palace of the governor was in Jerusalem, too. So it took some stones to head that way.

23 We finally get to Bethany, and it turns out he's there for a funeral. He had two girls there, two sisters, named Mary and Martha—sisters, wow, two at a time! I think he was a player, just like his dad with the Vermin Mary and her cousin Elisabeth. Anyway, this Mary and Martha, their brother had just died. His name was Lazarus.

24 So we track Jesus down at their house, and we get there right after he does. Martha's there, crying like crazy, and she's whining that Jesus could have saved Lazarus. I guess they'd heard about the raising the dead trick the apostles were doing, and I guess they believed it. So Martha, she begs Jesus to bring Lazarus back.

25 Jesus, he says, **Your brother shall rise again. I am the resurrection, and the life: he that believes in me, though he were dead, yet shall he live: And whoever lives and believes in me shall never die. Believe you this?**

26 There it was, the eternal life scam. So I was right, that's what they were selling. Martha, she says, sure I do, I believe it! And she calls Mary over, and Mary's crying like crazy, and now *she's* whining that Jesus could have saved Lazarus, too.

27 Jesus says, **Where have you laid him?** So they take him to the grave, it's a cave with a big rock covering the entrance, with a whole crowd of us following. And then Jesus says, **Take away the stone. Said I not to you, that, if you would believe, you should see the glory of God?**

28 But Martha, she says, "Man, hold on, he's gonna be stinkin', he's been dead for four days!" So maybe she's in on the trick, maybe she's not, I don't know.

29 Then Jesus looks up at the sky—that's when I knew something was up, just like when he was baptized, he acts like he's talking to someone up there—and he says, **Father, I thank you that you have heard me. And I know that you hear me always: but because of the people which stand by I said it, that they may believe that you have sent me.**

30 Then he raises his arms, and he says, **Lazarus, come forth!** And out pops Lazarus, wrapped in a tablecloth, with a napkin over his face. Lazarus, he stumbles around a little bit, I mean, who wouldn't after being dead for four days? (That was a nice touch.) And boy, did he stink. (Another nice touch.) And then Jesus says, **Loose him, and let him go.**

31 By now I'd seen everything, what with the thunder and the lightning and the fishes and the walking on water and all. Those were some impressive tricks,

let me tell you. But this one was nothing—I mean, how hard is it to pay some schmuck to hide in a cave for four days, then come out and dance a little jig?

32 The people went nuts. I couldn't figure out why, it wasn't like he sawed someone in half or anything. But by then, I had it all figured out: what are people most afraid of? Death, that's what. So you give them some hope that they can beat the Grim Reaper, and bippity boppity boop, you've got them!

33 What else could make someone sell everything they have and give it all to you? It was genius, trust me, absolute genius. People were just flocking to see Jesus. They really believed he was the Son of God, and the King of the Jews to boot. Gabriel, Jesus, the apostles, they must have been cleaning up, I mean, bigly.

34 By now, Jesus was known all over Judea and Samaria and Perea and Galilee, and who knows how far his story had spread to the east or north or south. But it had spread pretty far to the west, all the way to Rome, that I can tell you.

35 And raising Lazarus, that really raised a big stink with the Pharisees and the priests in Jerusalem. Jesus, he was getting too big for his britches, I mean, *way* too big.

36 The top dog among these priests, the high priest, he was this guy, Caiaphas. And Caiaphas was no fool, no fool at all. He knew which side his bread was buttered on, just like Herod Antipasto did. So Caiaphas, he tells the Pharisees and the other priests, look, we gotta whack this Jesus, and whack him fast. If we don't, the Romans will come and wipe us out. You know the Romans, they don't mess around.

37 Jesus should have known better. I told him, you mess with the emperor, and it's all over. I did my best—I helped keep him safe from Antipasto by spreading the rumor that he was born in Nazareth, not Bethlehem, and that King Herod the Great was born in Babylon.

38 I don't want to hurt my arm patting myself on the back, but that was brilliant! I have to give myself credit for that, nobody else will, the fake scribes won't give me credit for anything. I kept Antipasto off his back, and that kept him safe from Emperor Tiberius.

39 So now I figure I have more than one ace in the hole. Jesus already owes me for the whole Nazareth/Babylon thing that's keeping his head on his shoulders. Plus, I know the truth about his father—it's Gabriel, or I'm not Donald of Gaul. And I've finally seen right through his scam—as if I'm going to sell everything I have and give it to him!

40 He might find a million rubes to cough up their dough, but I won't be one of them. And if I wanted to, I could put the kibosh on the whole thing. I could spread the word all over that it was a scam. Hell, if I wanted to, I could rat him out to Herod Antipasto, and why not, to Tiberius Caesar, too. And that would be the end of the whole thing, absolutely the end.

41 Well maybe by now, he knows all that, because he's been giving me the slip, and this Jew holiday Passover is right around the corner, and I have all my guys out looking for him. Finally, we track him down, and me and my guys—I brought some muscle with me this time—we corner him in an alley in Bethany.

42 And I say, "*Jesus*, Jesus, where the hell have you been? I've been looking all over for you. Listen, I have to talk to you and your father, okay? I got a contract for you, right here. A hundred million sesterces. You heard me--*a hundred million!*"

43 That must've gotten his attention, let me tell you. He says, **A little while, and you shall not see me: and again, a little while, and you shall see me, because I go to the Father.** What a weird way of talking he had! So what's he telling me, that he's going to go talk to his father, then he'll come back?

44 I tell him, no, that's not how it works. I say, "No, no, I've had enough of this runaround stuff. Look, I know who your father is. It's Gabriel, and he was John's father, too. Take me to him, and I mean, right now, see?"

45 Jesus, he acts like he doesn't know what's going on. He says, **I seek not my own will, but the will of the Father which has sent me. There is another that bears witness of me: and I know that the witness which he witness of me is true. You sent for John, and he bore witness to the truth.**

46 **But I have greater witness than that of John: for the works which the Father has given me to finish, the same works that I do, bear witness**

of me, that the Father has sent me. And the Father himself, which sent me, has born witness of me.

47 I've heard the runaround before, I practically invented it, but this guy, he had it down. Witness this, bear that, John, the Father, me—he was talking in circles. But at least he seemed to be admitting who was who here—Gabriel was the boss, and John and Jesus were his lieutenants. So we were getting somewhere.

48 So I say, "Hold on, hold on. Let's get this straight. You can speak for your father, right?" And he says, **I have not spoken of myself; but the Father which sent me, he gave me a commandment, what I should say, and what I should speak.**

49 I say, "Yeah, I get that. But now I want to talk to *him*, got it? I'm onto the scam, you can drop the act. Don't worry, I'm not gonna drop a dime on you, okay? I just want in on it. And I can double, triple, quadruple your take—times ten, maybe even more. I have the pull in Rome, and in Jerusalem.

50 "Jesus Christ, man, I can take you all over the empire! I have inns, taverns, casinos, bath houses, theaters, from one end of the Mediterranean to the other. No more shitholes—you can work the Donald Bath, maybe even the Circus Maximus. You'll live like a king, a king I tell you, it'll be fantastic. Just take me to Gabriel."

51 So he says, **I am the way, the truth, and the life: no man comes to the Father, but by me.**

52 "Exactly!" I say. "Now we're getting somewhere. That's how it works with all the best families in Rome, and Sicily. You have to go through someone to get to the boss. So how about, you take me to Gabriel, and nobody gets hurt."

53 Most guys, with me and all that muscle, they would've folded like a toga right then and there. But not Jesus, not this guy. He says, **All things that the Father has, are mine. If you had known me, you should have known my Father also. I am come in my Father's name, and you receive me not.**

54 What a stubborn jerk he was, no respect at all. So I get right up in his face, and I take him by the front of his dirty smelly robe, and I'm looking down

at him—I'm, like, a head taller than he is—and I lay it right on the line: "Now listen, you little punk. You're gonna take me to see Gabriel, pronto, or else. And trust me, if I don't take care of you and your little gang of gypsies, the Romans will, and I'll see to it."

55 Then I give a little nod, and my guys, they close in and start breathing right down his skinny little neck. This guy had guts, let me tell you. He didn't flinch, he didn't back down, he just smiled that little smile of his and shook his head.

56 I was just about to slap that smile off his face, when, just my luck, these centurions walk by with some Roman soldiers and see us all huddled up in the alley. And one of the centurions, he says, "Hey you, what's going on back there?"

57 "Oh, nothing," I say, and I smooth out Jesus's robe, and we all back off. But these centurions, they have to stick their beaks into everybody's business, so they pick that little alley in that little shithole to take a little break.

58 What could we do? They were centurions. We'd have to wait until we could corner him again, we didn't have a choice.

59 But Jesus, he wasn't finished, he must've finally figured out that he had to deal with me, one way or another. So he says, **In my Father's house are many mansions: if it were not so, I would have told you. I go to prepare a place for you. And if I go and prepare a place for you, I will come again, and receive you to myself; that where I am, there you may also be.**

60 Well, how about that? He finally came around, he was going to arrange a meeting after all. Maybe not right then, or on my terms, but a meeting is a meeting. And just like I suspected, Crooked Gabriel had a bunch of mansions! Not just one, a bunch of them! They'd been cashing in all along, alright!

61 So I just nod my head, and I whisper, "Don't mess with me, kid. You got one day to arrange things. I'll be in town, I'll be easy to find. Just look for my chariot and my entourage. And we'll be keeping an eye on you, you can believe that."

62 Most guys would have left it at that, but no, not Jesus. He has to get in the last word. He says, **Do not think that I will accuse you to the Father: there is one that accuses you, even Moses. For had you believed Moses, you would have believed me, for he wrote of me. But if you believe not his writings, how shall you believe my words?**

63 With everything he owed me, and with me in on the whole scam, he talks to me like that? Like he's going to rat me out to his dad? Like I'm afraid of him, or Gabriel, or any army they could bring against me, Donald of Gaul?

64 And did he really still expect me to buy into the whole Son of God schtick, or the Ten Commandments, or this Jew prophet Moses's predictions about some phony savior? Holy Moly! Give me a break, I wasn't born yesterday.

65 So now we watch him. I put my best guys on him, they're following him everywhere, and I still have my man on the inside, deep on the inside. He wasn't going to give me the slip again, no way.

66 I was getting close, I could almost taste it.

9 So what does this little guy do, this Jesus so-called Christ? Does he go talk to Gabriel? No! He gets these twelve apostles together, and what else, he starts talking. Blah blah blah, yadda yadda yadda, he never shuts up!

2 Only now, I have my man on the inside, and we have one of my secretaries—not like those hot numbers from Sodom and Gomorrah, no way, we didn't need a distraction—we have one of my secretaries on the inside playing a servant. She brings them water, she cleans the dishes, she washes their robes, whatever she needs to do to stay on the inside, she does. And she writes down everything they say, she writes down every word.

3 And right off the bat, Jesus, he goes against his word. His word to me, Donald of Gaul. He's not going to Gabriel's mansions at all, he's heading to

Jerusalem, right into the lion's mouth. And get this, he knows it! It's like he's setting himself up!

4 He tells these apostles, he says, **Behold, we go up to Jerusalem: and the Son of man shall be betrayed to the chief priests and the scribes, and they shall condemn him to death, and shall deliver him to the Gentiles to mock him, and to scourge him, and to spit upon him, and to crucify him: and the third day he shall rise again.**

5 When word of that got back to me, boy was I steaming. I figured he was up to something, something big, and considering how the Pharisees and Romans were close on his heels, I thought I knew what it was. He was trying to get himself killed, that's what—or at least, to make it look like he got himself killed. "I am the resurrection, and the life," he said. "The third day he shall rise again," he said.

6 He and those apostles, they'd been raising the dead already, and probably making a fortune because of it. What if he could make it look like he'd raised *himself* from the dead? That would be the best advertising they could get. Word would spread all over, and this scam of theirs, it would take off like crazy, believe me, it would really take off.

7 On his last day in Bethany, he throws a dinner party. Mary's there, and Martha's there, and of course, Lazarus is there. All these hillbillies from the countryside, they come to see Jesus and Lazarus, who he supposedly brought back from the dead. Not a bad promotion, not bad at all, so I go to see it myself.

8 Mary, she takes some ointment—it was Spikenard, the best brand there is, I import it from the east for my inns—and she starts to oil Jesus's feet with it. That was sexy, let me tell you, I wish she'd have done that for me! So she rubs it into his feet, then she wipes his feet with her hair. Oo-la-la, that girl was something!

9 Now Judas Iscariot, I mentioned him before, he says, "Hey, Jesus, that's some high-end stuff you got there. Why wasn't this ointment sold for three hundred pence, and given to the poor?" Don't be fooled, Judas didn't care for

the poor any more than I do. He was just razzing Jesus, probably because I was there and he knew we were on the outs.

10 And Jesus says, **Let her alone. Against the day of my burying has she kept this. For the poor you will always have with you; but me you will not always have. She has done what she could: she is come beforehand to anoint my body to the burying.**

11 I'm no dummy, I can read between the lines. "Against the day of my burying," he says. "Anoint my body to the burying." I was right. Jesus was setting himself up for the biggest magic trick of all time, the one that would bring the whole scam to fruitation. He was going to get himself killed, then bring himself back to life again.

12 Juno and Jupiter, these guys were something else! What a show *that* would be!

13 By now, Jesus had hundreds of people all around him, day and night, night and day, following him wherever he went. I couldn't get to him if I wanted to, and dammit, by then, I'd just about had it with him. Plus, I couldn't afford to get on the bad side of Caiaphas, or Antipasto, or Tiberius (Praise Caesar!) anyway.

14 If he wouldn't cut me in, to hell with him! I could always get my own magicians and do my own shows. It was just magic, it wasn't brain surgery or anything. His apostles, they'd work for way less than a hundred million sesterces, that much I knew.

15 If *he* knew what *I* knew, maybe he wouldn't have been so cocky. I knew the Pharisees were planning on killing him, and they were thinking about killing Lazarus, too. And there were plenty of people back in Rome who knew about Jesus, and some of them wanted to see a "miracle," and some of them wanted to see an execution.

16 So there were these good-for-nothing Greeks at the dinner in Bethany. I'll give them credit, the Greeks, they can teach and write like nobody's business, but teaching and writing, what is that really good for? And they went to

Philip—he was an apostle—and to Andrew, another apostle, and said they wanted to talk to Jesus.

17 And Jesus, he says to bring them on in. What the hell, he won't see me, Donald of Gaul, but he'll see these greasy Greeks he doesn't even know? And for some reason, he chooses that moment to get up on his high horse. He says,

18 **The hour is come, that the Son of man should be glorified. Truly, truly, I say to you, Except a corn of wheat falls into the ground and dies, it abides alone: but if it dies, it brings forth much fruit. Father, the hour is come; glorify your Son, that your Son may glorify you; and you have given him power over all flesh, that he should give eternal life to as many as you have given him.**

19 Now he's looking up at the sky again, and he's talking to his father, so I start looking around for Crooked Gabriel, for someone who looks like Jesus and John. But if he was smart, Gabriel, and he was, he'd be wearing a disguise. Maybe he was one of those Greeks, who knows. Anyway, here's Jesus, talking about dying, and living forever, and all that poppycock:

20 **Now is my soul troubled; and what shall I say? Father, save me from this hour: but for this cause came I to this hour. Father, glorify your name.**

21 "This is it," I say to myself, "He's acting like he's talking to NoWay again." And sure enough, just like the day when I first met Jesus and John the Batshit, here comes this voice out of the sky. So that's when I knew for sure the ventriloquist was Jesus. I have to say, he was pissing me off bigly, but boy, was he good! The best ventriloquist I ever heard, it was terrific.

22 And this voice, it says, ***"I have glorified it, and will glorify it again."*** And Jesus answers back—he was answering himself, you know, like a comic talking to a doll on his knee—he answers back, **This voice came not because of me, but for your own sakes. Now is the judgment of this world: now shall the prince of this world be cast out. And I, if I be lifted up from the earth, will draw all men to me.**

23 So there it was. He was going to get himself killed, then rise up again, be "lifted up from the earth." Venus and Vesuvius, what an act that would be!

I figured, he must have some priests and scribes in on it, maybe even a centurion or two.

24 Crooked Gabriel had probably paid them off, they probably had the whole thing planned to a "T."

25 But if they did that, where would that leave me? Sure, I could pay off an apostle or two, put my own show on the road, maybe pick up a little scratch here and there at my properties. But Jesus and Gabriel, with this come-back-from-the-dead trick, they'd practically have a monopoly on the whole traveling preacher racket. Things were falling apart, and I wasn't happy, I have to tell you.

26 So now Jesus heads towards Jerusalem, because Passover is coming, this big Jew holiday. And when he gets to the Mount of Olives, he tells a couple of his flunkies to go find him a donkey, pronto. He says, **Go into the village, in which you shall find a colt tied, on which man has never sat: set him loose, and bring him here.**

27 **And if any man asks you, Why do you set loose the colt? Thus shall you say to him, Because the Lord has need of him.** And off they go, because "the Lord" told them to, if you can believe it. And there are hundreds, maybe thousands of people following him by now, it's crazy.

28 In a while, the two apostles, here they come with this little donkey colt. It wasn't even full grown, and the other apostles, they start throwing their clothes on it, like a saddle. And Jesus hops up there, like he's a general on a black stallion or something—you should see my horses, I have the best horses, they're fantastic—but Jesus, he's just a dirty little magician riding a dirty little ass!

29 Well these people, they've been flimflammed but good, and they're lining the roads, and throwing robes and scarves and palm branches onto the road in front of him. And they're yelling, "Blessed be the King that comes in the name of the Lord," and "Hosanna! Blessed is the King of Israel."

30 Yeah, right, the King. The King, my ass. I knew that wouldn't set well with the Pharisees, or the priests, or the Romans. Just tell it to the emperor, see what that gets you.

31 The stones on this guy! He rides right into downtown Jerusalem, with people filling the streets, and goes straight to the Temple. Now these Jews, I don't think much of their temple, it's got no flair—just a big cube of rocks as far as I can tell. But they love this temple, they do everything there, it's like, the center of their lives.

32 Jesus, he goes into the Temple, and (you guessed it) he starts talking. He's preaching about this, and he's preaching about that, and he keeps saying that Moses and Elijah and Isaiah and John and all those so-called prophets said a savior would come. And now, he says here I am, the Christ! Ta-da! What an ego on this guy, you have to be kidding me.

33 Now maybe I've been talking to the priests and Pharisees, and maybe I haven't. But I know they want to get rid of Jesus. So maybe they pay some folks, you know, to throw some loaded questions at the guy. I had nothing to do with it, the fake scribes can say whatever they want to.

34 Here's Jesus, preaching in the Temple, and someone shouts out, "Hey, Jesus, why do you hang out with all these whores and thieves and losers?" And Jesus, he says,

35 **They that are whole need not a physician, but they that are sick. But go and learn what that means, I will have mercy and not sacrifice: for I am not come to call the righteous, but sinners to repentance.**

36 Okay, pretty good answer. Then someone else shouts out, "Yo, Jesus, why do you and your apostles work on the Sabbath, healing lepers and plucking corn and whatnot?" And Jesus says,

37 **Have you not read in the law, how that on the Sabbath days the priests in the Temple profane the Sabbath, and are blameless? But I say to you, that in this place is one greater than the Temple. But if you had known what this means, you would not have condemned the guiltless. For the Son of man is Lord even of the Sabbath day.**

38 Not bad, not bad, he was pretty sharp, let me tell you. He had an answer for everything. Then someone else shouts out, "How 'bout this, Jesus, why

don't you and your apostles wash your hands before you eat bread, like you're supposed to, huh? How 'bout that?" And he says,

39 That which goes into the mouth does not defile a man, but that which comes out of the mouth. Those things which proceed out of the mouth, come forth from the heart; and it is they that defile the man. For out of the heart proceed evil thoughts, murders, adulteries, fornications, thefts, false witness, blasphemies: these are the things which defile a man, but to eat with unwashed hands does not defile a man.

40 I swear, just when he was nailing down that list—the adulteries, fornications, thefts, false witness—he picked me out of the crowd and looked right at me. He looked me right in the eye, even though I was in a corner halfway across the Temple. The nerve of that guy!

41 The temple priests and the Pharisees, and Caiaphas, they're starting to pull their hair out. No matter what they do, Jesus does them one better. He was right up in their faces, like I said, trying to get himself whacked.

42 The next day, he comes to the Temple again, and it's so full of people you can hardly move. Caiaphas and the temple priests are shaking in their boots, they just can't seem to trip this guy up.

43 And there are some Romans there, they worked for Pontius Pilate—he was the Roman Governor of Judea, he had a palace right there in Jerusalem, it was built by Herod the Great. The Romans, they were getting pretty worried, too. The last thing they needed was some radical getting the people riled up and making them look bad in Rome.

44 But instead of preaching, what does Jesus do? He goes over to these tables, where people are selling sheep and doves, and changing money, and he makes a little whip, and he starts whipping these jokers like nobody's business. He knocks over their tables, and ka-ching! Money goes spilling all over the place, and doves go flying all over the place, and sheep are running around in circles.

45 And Jesus, it was the only time I ever saw him mad, he says, **Take these things away from here; make not my Father's house a house of merchandise.**

Is it not written, My house shall be called of all nations a house of prayer? But you have made it a den of thieves.

46 Now maybe I've been talking to the Romans, and maybe I haven't. But I know they want to get rid of Jesus. And as soon as they get rid of him, maybe I can start working on these apostles to sign up with me and get my own shows on the road. The hospitality business, it needs entertainers, and these guys, they weren't Jesus, but they were good.

47 Take this guy Peter, Aint Peter, he was the number two guy, after Jesus. I figure, maybe he wants to move up to number one and get that big contract that Jesus keeps throwing back in my face. Nobody wants to be number two, am I right?

48 But if Jesus pulls off the whole getting whacked and coming-back-from-the-dead trick, it's all over. They'll all stick with him, he'll be the biggest act in the empire. I was running out of time, I had to sign Jesus now or not at all.

49 So the money changers, they're scrambling to pick up all their coins, and this murmur is going through the crowd. The Roman big shots are over in a corner, shaking their heads and whispering to each other. I give this one priest, he's on my payroll, see, I give him a nudge.

50 He steps up, and he clears his throat real loud, and everyone's looking his way. And he says to Jesus, "Master, we know that you are true, and care for no man: for you regard not the person of men, but teach the way of God in truth." And then he pauses, and the people are all nodding their heads.

51 Then he throws a glance at the Romans, and he looks Jesus right in the eye, and he says, "Is it lawful to give tribute to Caesar, or not? Shall we give, or shall we not give?"

52 Now everybody's murmuring, and the Romans prick up their ears. What's he going to do? If he says "Yes, pay up," he looks like a chump. If he says "No, don't pay up," he has Tiberius Caesar to deal with. Yahweh, No Way, he was screwed either way!

53 Jesus, he doesn't flinch, I have to give the guy credit. He knows what they're up to. He says, **Why tempt me, you hypocrites? Bring me a penny, that I may see it. Whose is this image, and superscription?** The people, they know who's on a penny. And they all say, "Caesar! That's Caesar!"

54 And Jesus looks around, nods his head, and says, **Render to Caesar the things that are Caesar's, and to God the things that are God's.** The people, they're buzzing, they can see what's happening, and they like it.

55 But what a wishy-washy answer that was! I say to myself, "Jesus Effing Christ, he should have been a politician." The Romans, they see how slippery this guy is, so they give up and head back to the palace.

56 Then this lawyer, I think he was one of the Pharisees, he says, "Master, which is the greatest commandment in the law?"

57 And Jesus says, **You shall love the Lord your God with all your heart, and with all your soul, and with all your mind. This is the first great commandment. And the second is like it, You shall love your neighbor as yourself. On these two commandments hang all the law and all the prophets.**

58 The people, they loved that, now they were cheering and clapping. The guy knew how to work a crowd, you can believe that. But love your neighbor as yourself? What if your neighbor is a jerk? What if you want his wife? What if he's your enemy? You can't love your enemy, that doesn't make any sense, like I tried to tell him before.

59 Any good performer knows, you have to end on a high note, and the people, by now they were clapping like crazy. So Jesus, he takes a little bow, and he walks right out of The Temple with some apostles, and I fall in right behind them, with hundreds of people scrambling to talk to him or touch him. It was a zoo, I can tell you that.

60 I hadn't given up on Jesus, not just yet. I had a proposition to make. Passover was just two days away. I figured, if they're going to get the biggest audience they can, that's the time to do it. They probably had something big planned, maybe even the grand finale, where he gets himself whacked.

61 So I pull aside one of the apostles and offer to cater the whole Passover supper—the best food, the best wine, the prettiest serving girls, the whole nine yards. And I tell him to run it by Judas Iscariot, he knows where to find me. Just name the place, and I'll have everything ready and waiting.

62 That's when I hear one of the apostles say, "Master, that's some temple, ain't it?" And Jesus, he answers, **See you these great buildings? There shall not be one stone upon another, that shall not be thrown down.**

63 There it was, in plain words—he wasn't just going to put on a show, he was planning to throw down the Temple! A revolt! And I had it straight out of his mouth.

64 Well, that changed everything. I couldn't have anything to do with him now. I had to do business with the Romans, I had to kiss their asses up one side and down the other, okay? If they knew I was in with Jesus, I could lose everything!

65 Two days until Passover, that was all I had, and there was plenty of work to be done, plenty of work.

66 I was going to make this a supper to be remembered. And maybe, if the Pharisees and the Romans had their way—and it wouldn't be my fault if they did, I had nothing to do with that—it was going to be Jesus's last.

10 After he said that about throwing down the Temple, Little Jesus—that's what I started calling him, he was barely three cubits tall—Little Jesus took the apostles up to the Mount of Olives again. Not a bad spot, the Mount of Olives, it has a great view. I could make it a first-class development if I could get my hands on it, believe me.

2 Anyway, they're up on this mountain, and the apostles, they're worried. I figure they're in on the coming-back-from-the-dead scam, and they know it won't be so easy to pull off.

3 So a few of them—Aint Peter and his brother Andrew, and the brothers James and John—they call Jesus off to the side and ask him what the hell is going on. Lucky for me, one of my secretaries is there, and she writes down what he says. It was one helluva magic trick he was planning, that I can tell you!

4 Jesus, he calls out to the other apostles, and he says to all twelve of them, **The Son of Man is about to be betrayed into the hands of men, and they will kill him. And after he is killed, he will rise on the third day.**

5 The magic trick to end all magic tricks. Dead for three days, then come back to life. Then they ask him what will come next, and you have to hear what he said. It was crazy, I mean, big league crazy. It was like he was mixing magic and prophecy or something. He says,

6 **Take heed lest any man deceive you. And many false prophets shall arise, and shall deceive many. And you shall hear of wars and rumours of wars, for nation shall rise against nation, and kingdom against kingdom: and there shall be earthquakes in divers places, and there shall be famines and pestilences. And because iniquity shall abound, the love of many shall wax cold.**

7 **But before all these, take heed to yourselves: for they will lay hands on you, and persecute you, delivering you up to councils and into the synagogues and prisons, and you shall be beaten; and some of you shall they cause to be put to death.**

8 **After that tribulation, the sun shall be darkened, and the moon shall not give her light, and the stars shall fall from heaven.**

9 **And then shall they see the Son of man coming in the clouds with great power and glory. And he shall send his angels with a great sound of a trumpet, and they shall gather together his elect from the four winds, from one end of heaven to the other.**

10 Mars and Minerva, what was that all about? Wars and earthquakes, no sun or moon or stars, and then he'll come storming out of heaven with a bunch of angels. Who'd believe that kind of claptrap? It was ridiculous, no magician could pull that off, not even Jesus could do that.

11 Beating and killing some apostles, that you could believe, they were practically begging for it.

12 He wasn't finished, though, not by a long shot. Here he was, calling himself the Son of man, and the King of the Jews, and the Son of God. But I think he was losing it, I mean, bigly. He starts calling himself "the King" and talking about his "throne." It was like he wanted the Romans to come and chop off his head!

13 He says, **When the Son of man shall come in his glory, and all the holy angels with him, then shall he sit upon the throne of his glory: And before him shall be gathered all nations: and he shall separate them one from another, as a shepherd divides his sheep from the goats. And he shall set the sheep on his right hand, but the goats on the left.**

14 **Then shall the King say to them on his right hand, Come, you blessed of my Father, inherit the kingdom he prepared for you from the foundation of the world. For I was hungry, and you gave me meat: I was thirsty, and you gave me drink: I was a stranger, and you took me in: naked, and you clothed me: I was sick, and you visited me: I was in prison, and you came to me.**

15 **Then shall the righteous answer him, saying, Lord, when did we see you hungry, and fed you? Or thirsty, and gave you drink? When did we see you a stranger and took you in? Or naked and clothed you? And when did we see you sick, or in prison, and came to you?**

16 **And the King shall answer and say to them, Truly I say to you, Inasmuch as you have done it to one of the least of these my brothers and sisters, you have done it to me.**

17 **Then shall he say also to them on the left hand, Depart from me, you cursed, into everlasting fire, prepared for the devil and his angels: For I was hungry, and you gave me no meat: I was thirsty, and you gave me no drink: I was a stranger, and you took me not in: naked, and you clothed me not: sick, and in prison, and you visited me not.**

18 Then shall they also answer him, saying, Lord, when did we see you hungry, or thirsty, or a stranger, or naked, or sick, or in prison, and did not minister to you?

19 Then shall he answer them, saying, Truly, I say to you, Inasmuch as you did it not to one of the least of these my brothers and sisters, you did it not to me. And these shall go into everlasting punishment: but the righteous into life eternal.

20 Well, that was some speech, let me tell you. He was giving them a pep talk, right before the big finale, and laying it on thick. Stick with me, he tells them, and you get to live forever in heaven. Don't, and you'll be punished, and I mean, forever, in hell!

21 What a way to close the deal when you're scamming your marks out of everything they own: if you say no, you'll go to hell, forever. So that was it: Damnation. Now *that's* a protection racket, let me tell you, the ultimate protection racket. That was the final piece to the scam, the Ultimate Con.

22 I didn't get that schtick about "the least of these my brothers and sisters," though. Come on, who gives a crap about a bunch of losers? If you can't feed yourself, or get decent clothes—like John the Batshit—that's your problem, not mine.

23 Slums, beggars, refugees, homeless people—who needs them? What good are they? They're just a load the rest of us have to carry, they drain the treasury, they devalue good property. And they look like crap, I hate to even have to look at them, it's disgraceful. And they stink, too. These aren't people, these are animals.

24 So Jesus, he's going to get himself killed, or make it look like he got himself killed, and then three days later, he's going to rise up again, and then all hell's going to break loose, with earthquakes and lightning and beatings and such.

25 And then after a while, he's going to come back, right out of heaven, and divvy up the good guys and the bad guys, and that's when all those suckers

will get their condo in paradise and their eternal life. And the rest of us will be damned, and I guess, go to hell.

26 It was nuts, a total hoax, I mean, who would fall for that bullshit? But some people will believe anything, let me tell you. I have people at my rallies, I could stand in the middle of the Appian Way and kill somebody, and I wouldn't lose any followers, that's how it is with some people. It's, like, incredible.

27 If I was one of those apostles, I would have hightailed it out of there, right then and there. But these guys, these losers, they're eating it up, at least eleven of them are. He called them sheep, and what did they do? They said, "Baa! Baa!"

28 Then he tells them, he says, **You know that after two days is the feast of Passover, and the Son of man is betrayed to be crucified.**

29 Crucified? That was the second time he said he was going to be crucified. When I heard that, I knew the whole thing was rigged. How could he know how he was going to die, unless it was all a setup?

30 It was a setup, alright. That Crooked Gabriel, he was pulling some strings, maybe in the Temple, maybe even with the Romans. He had the money, I was sure of that, they'd been cashing in all along, and leaving me on the outs.

31 Thank goodness I had my people on the inside, it came in handy, real handy. Two days later, Little Jesus tells two of these apostles, he says, **Go and prepare us the Passover, that we may eat. Go into the city, and there shall you meet a man bearing a pitcher of water: follow him into the house where he enters.**

32 **And you shall say to the goodman of the house, The Master says to you, Where is the guestchamber, where I shall eat the Passover with my disciples? And he shall show you a large upper room, furnished and prepared; there make ready for us.**

33 So I have a guy in Jerusalem ready and waiting with a pitcher of water, and he leads them to a house I rented there for the occasion, and I put the cater-

ing crew on it right away. We make some bread, a nice bean stew, some herbs, a fish sauce, and for the main course—what else, lamb!

34 Yeah, lamb! These sheep of Jesus's, I was going to turn them into cannibals. So I tell my guys, "Hey look, these sheep are going to eat lamb, like a bunch of cannibals in Ethiopia!" They laugh it up, they always laugh at my jokes. I have the best jokes, they're fantastic.

35 And wine, there had to be wine, it was a feast. I guess we could have just served water and let Jesus do his little presto-chango, water-into-wine trick, but no, he had to save that for his little act.

36 There are thirteen of them, and of course Jesus, he thinks he's the King of the World by now. So I set up this long table, and I put them all on the same side, with Jesus in the middle, just like he was Caesar sitting at the head table at a banquet. Nice goblets, silver plates—I give them the works—and a special platter that I got from Herod Antipasto. (Maybe it was Salome's, if you know what I mean.)

37 Sure enough, before too long here they come, and we seat them all on that one side. They don't know I'm there—at least twelve of them don't—but I'm behind a curtain right in front of them, where I can see and hear everything.

38 For some reason, they sit in threes, six on Jesus's left and six on his right, like they're posing for a painting, and they start drinking and carrying on. John—he looked just like a woman if you ask me—and Peter and Judas are on his right, and he has a James on each side. You should have seen them sitting there like they were Caesar and his cabinet.

39 Judas, he spills the salt, the idiot, and Peter, he's ranting and holding a knife behind Judas's back. Jesus, he's all sad and quiet, probably thinking about this trick he was about to try to pull off. But then he hushes them all up, and he says, **Truly I say to you, One of you which eats with me shall betray me.** Well, they all look each other up and down and start arguing, which one of them is the rat?

40 Then it gets really weird. Jesus, he breaks up a loaf of bread and passes it around, and he says, **Take, eat; this is my body.** Then he pours some wine and

passes it around, and he says, **This is my blood of the new testament, which is shed for many.**

41 **Truly, truly, I say to you, He that believes in me has everlasting life. Except you eat the flesh of the Son of man, and drink his blood, you have no life in you. Who eats my flesh and drinks my blood, has eternal life.**

42 The nerve of this guy, here he was, mocking my joke about cannibals. He must've had a guy on the inside with *me,* damn him. Me, Donald of Gaul! How else could he be in on the joke? I mean, it's not like someone's just going to up and talk about people eating his body and drinking his blood. And I guess he was eating his own body and drinking his own blood, too. What the hell, that's nuts!

43 Would you believe, from there on out, these sheep who follow Jesus, thousands of them, they eat bread and drink wine and pretend they're eating his flesh and drinking his blood, all because of a joke of mine. I'm not making that up, anyone will tell you.

44 As soon as they've had their fill of Jesus, they sing a little song, a hymn, and off they go again, without paying the tab—the old dine and dash. Not even a thank you. And a tip? Nothing, not a plug quadrans!

45 Like I said before, the apostles schlepped all over the empire without any money, and they didn't even get expense accounts. They stayed and ate wherever they could, bumming off whoever was fool enough to put them up. If they don't pay or leave a tip, who can blame them, they've got no money.

46 But Jesus, he and Gabriel probably had millions stashed away, maybe billions (but not as much as me, I was worth twelve, maybe fifteen billion sesterces.) They could have paid the bill, or at least left a tip. I can't stand dead-beats, nobody wants to pay their share anymore.

47 Off they go to the Mount of Olives again, and Jesus, he's still talking, go figure. According to my guy on the inside, he says, **All of you shall be offended because of me this night: for it is written, I will smite the shepherd, and the sheep of the flock shall be scattered abroad. But after I am risen again, I will go before you into Galilee.**

48 Aint Peter, he's not buying it. He says, "Though all men shall be offended because of you, yet will I never be offended." Jesus shakes his head and says, **Truly I say to you, that this night, before the cock crows, you shall deny me thrice.**

49 Well Peter, I'll give him credit, he was a loyal soldier. He says, "Though I should die with you, yet will I not deny you." And the apostles all say, "Yeah, me too!" That's not how it turned out, though, not even close. Talk is cheap, that's what I say.

50 Then Jesus leads them to the foot of the mountain, to a garden called Gethsemane, and he says, **Sit here, while I shall pray.** And he takes Peter and the Sons of Thunder, his pets, aside, and he starts whining and crying about how scared he is.

51 Like, maybe he was worried his little scheme would fall apart or something, and he'd wind up crucified for real, I don't know. I didn't have anything to do with that, don't believe what the fake scribes say, they're very dishonest people.

52 He tells them, **My soul is exceedingly sorrowful, even until death: tarry here, and watch.** But the apostles, they can't even keep a watch, they fall asleep, so he wakes them up. And he says to Aint Peter, he says, **Peter, do you sleep? Could not you watch one hour? Watch, and pray, lest you enter into temptation. The spirit indeed is willing, but the flesh is weak.**

53 They fall asleep again, and he wakes them up again. But then they fall asleep one more time. Jesus, he gives up on them. He says, **Sleep on now, and take your rest.** But after a while, he says, **Behold, the hour is at hand, and the Son of man is betrayed into the hands of sinners. Rise, let us be going: behold, he is at hand that betrays me.**

54 Sure enough, here comes Judas Iscariot, with a whole mob of Jews and Romans, all of them carrying swords and staves and ready to rumble. Judas led them right to him.

55 I didn't have anything to do with it, trust me, but I heard that the Pharisees had a secret code for the leaders of the mob—that whoever Judas kissed,

that was Jesus, and they should grab him and hold on tight. So Judas walks up to Jesus, and he says, "Master, Master!" And he gives him a smack right on the cheek.

56 Jesus says, **Friend, why have you come? Judas, do you betray the Son of man with a kiss?**

57 Now, there were hundreds of people in this mob, and some of them were my people, and I was there, too. Not that I had anything to do with it, it's just that my people were keeping tabs on Jesus and the apostles, and with all my businesses there, I had people all over Jerusalem. Just a coincidence, that's all.

58 Hundreds in the mob, against Jesus and eleven wimpy apostles. Boy would that have been something to see at any arena in the empire! The Sons of Thunder would have been pretty quiet, I can tell you that. They would have been torn limb from limb.

59 By now, the priests have come, and it's not looking good. But Aint Peter, he grabs a sword, and wham! He chops off the ear of one of the high priest's servants! Give the guy credit, he had guts.

60 Maybe it was part of the act, maybe it wasn't, but Jesus doesn't want any trouble. He just wants to get this whole come-back-from-the-dead trick over with. So he touches this guy's ear, and bingo! It's healed. That was some trick, that ear thing, the guy was good.

61 Then Jesus, he looks at the priests, and he says, **Do you come out, as against a thief, with swords and staves? When I was daily with you in the Temple, you stretched forth no hands against me: but this is your hour, and the power of darkness. The scriptures must be fulfilled.**

62 The apostles, when they hear that, ten of them, they run like hell, let me tell you, and they don't look back. What a bunch of losers. Like I said before, they were weak, totally weak. Only Aint Peter, he was the most loyal one, he sticks around at the back of the mob. And they take Jesus and haul him off to the palace of the high priest, Caiaphas.

63 Jesus was really in a pickle now! As far as I could tell, he thought he had the whole thing worked out. He thought he had some people in the Temple, maybe even some Pharisees, on his payroll to help him fake his death and the whole coming-back-from-the-dead thing.

64 Maybe he thought he had a centurion or two on his payroll, too. There was this one centurion in Capernaum who supposedly had so much faith, that Jesus healed his servant, sight unseen. So he had at least one centurion on his side for sure. Maybe he had more, like the ones that saved his ass from me in that alley in Bethany.

65 But these guys who had Jesus now, and Caiaphas for sure, they weren't in on the scam. *That* I can tell you.

66 I'll bet Jesus was shaking in his sandals! I'll bet he wished he'd signed a contract with Donald of Gaul then! I'm not going to say he got what was coming to him, I won't say that. But maybe he got what was coming to him.

67 They drag him in front of Caiaphas, and all the temple priests are there, and a bunch of scribes and elders. And they start asking him questions. They're trying to trip him up again, to get him to say the wrong thing, something illegal. They want to execute him and be done with him for good, but he's not saying a thing, he's too smart for them.

68 A lot of people are there, and they're saying all kinds of things against Jesus. Like, that he said he was a king, and the Son of God. And that he was perverting the nation, and forbidding people to give tribute to Caesar. But they were all nobodies, and they couldn't get their stories straight, and even Caiaphas, he didn't want to execute Jesus without some good evidence.

69 Finally, these two guys come up, and one of them says, "This fellow said, 'I am able to destroy the Temple of God, and to build it back again in three days.'" He was a hillbilly, a real nobody. But his buddy backs him up, he says, "Yeah, that's right. I heard it, too."

70 Well, I'd heard Jesus at the Temple myself, saying, "There shall not be one stone upon another that shall not be thrown down." And I knew there was

no way to build a temple in three days, even Donald of Gaul couldn't do that! So I look at Caiaphas, and I nod my head.

71 What can I say, it was the truth, and no one loves the truth more than me, Donald of Gaul. And so Caiaphas, now he has two witnesses, and he knows I'll back them up. But it still wasn't enough. Caiaphas, he's getting hot under the collar, and he gets up in Jesus's face, and he says, real serious like, "Are you the Christ, the Son of the Blessed?"

72 And Jesus, he finally cracks. He says, **I am: and you shall see the Son of man sitting on the right hand of power, and coming in the clouds of heaven. Hereafter shall the Son of man sit on the right hand of God.**

73 Caiaphas, he finally has what he wants. He starts ripping at his robes, and he yells, "What need we further witnesses? You have heard the blasphemy: what think you?"

74 Well, that was it. The mob, it's full of Pharisees and priests and scribes and all their friends, and they've had it with Jesus. Lots of my people are there, too, and maybe they agree. Not because of me, of course—it's not like I control anyone, I let people think for themselves, that's what *I* do.

75 People start yelling that Jesus should be put to death, and they start to spit on him and push him around. Some servants, they start slapping his face, left and right. An officer from the Temple, he slaps him, too, and hard, you can hear it clear across the palace. Boy was he turning the other cheek then, back and forth, back and forth, he was like a punching bag, pow, pow, pow!

76 I was in the palace when that happened, I was near the fireplace, and who do I see but Aint Peter sitting there warming himself. And a maid, she recognizes him, and she says, "This man was with Jesus." And Aint Peter, he says, "Woman, I know him not," and he goes out onto the porch.

77 Then a guy out on the porch, it was the guy whose ear Peter chopped off, he says, "Did I not see you in the garden with Jesus?" And Aint Peter says, "Man, I know not what you say." And he leaves the porch.

78 Then another guy says, "Of a truth, this fellow was also with Jesus: for this is a Galilean." And Aint Peter says, "Man, I am not." So he denied Jesus three times, just like Jesus said he would.

79 Just then, a cock crows, just like Jesus said, and Peter starts cussing and crying. I don't know if that was magic, I mean, it wasn't like a dove flew down onto his shoulder or anything. But you have to admit, that cock crowing just then, that was one funny coincidence.

80 They haul Jesus to a cell and lock him up, waiting to bring him the next day to the Roman Governor, Pontius Pilate. (I called him "Pompous Pilates," he should have owned a gym somewhere instead of being the governor.)

81 Herod Antipasto, he was in Jerusalem, too. So I go to see him, and we make plans to go to Pompous Pilates's palace the next day. Caiaphas and the temple priests, they want Jesus dead, and since he's been talking about his own crucifixion, I guess that's what they're going to give him.

82 I figured, he and Gabriel, they'd had a crucifixion all planned out, and he had some people on the inside to fake it, or he never would have come to Jerusalem raising hell and getting in their faces in the first place.

83 Fat lot of good that did him! Now he was in the hands of the Pharisees and the Romans, and they had a cross, a *real* cross, with his name on it.

84 It was going to take some strong magic, some very strong magic, to get out of *that*.

11 The next morning, they take Jesus to Pompous Pilates's palace, which was close to the Temple. Not a bad palace, it had some nice touches, but nowhere near as nice as mine in Rome. I have summer homes nicer than Pompous Pilates's palace, way nicer.

2 Judas Iscariot, don't ask me how I know, but he took thirty pieces of silver to betray Jesus. Thirty pieces of silver! What a fool, the Romans were

offering fifty talents of gold—that's what I hear, I didn't have anything to do with it—and Judas did it for thirty pieces of silver. Someone made a nice profit, believe me.

3 So Judas, he's feeling guilty, and he tries to give the silver back to the chief priests, but they won't take it. He throws the silver down on the floor, and walks off, and from what I hear, he goes and hangs himself from a tree. I thought he was alright before that, but he was just another loser, a total disgrace.

4 Now Pilates, he says to Jesus, "Are you the King of the Jews?" Jesus, the tough guy, all he says is, **You say so.** All those times he called himself the Son of God and the King of the Jews, and now, he clams up. What a wimp. I would've said, "Hell yeah, that's me, King of the Jews," that's what I would've done.

5 Then this jury of priests, called the Sanhedrin, starts asking Jesus questions and accusing him of claiming to be the Son of God. He was guilty, no doubt! I'd seen it all myself, right from the beginning, at that sewer, the Jordan River, with John the Batshit.

6 Jesus doesn't say a word, he doesn't answer any of them. He just stands there with that sad little smile of his, looking at the ground, just like he did every time I tried to get him to come work for me. Me, Donald of Gaul. No one says no to me, no one.

7 Pilates, he says, "Answer you nothing? Behold how many things they witness against you." Jesus still doesn't say anything, and Pilates, his eyes get big, like he's seeing some marvel—he's used to people kissing his shoes, see—and he turns to the priests and says, "I find no fault in this man."

8 The priests all start whining, they say, "He stirs up the people, teaching throughout all Jewry, beginning from Galilee to this place." Pilates, he's trying to weasel his way out of it, see, and he knows Galilee is Herod Antipasto's turf. So he sends Jesus and the priests over to Antipasto, who wasn't far away.

9 Antipasto, he asks a bunch of questions, and he asks to see a magic trick, or a miracle, or whatever you call this guy's little act. Jesus still won't talk, and he's not in the mood to do any magic. So Antipasto and his soldiers put a nice

purple robe on the guy, they push him around some, they razz him a little bit, and they send him back to Pilates.

10 Pilates and Herod, they'd been at each other's throats before that. But Herod appreciated being let in on it, so they kissed and made up afterwards. I didn't have anything to do with that, okay? I didn't need either of those guys, they meant nothing to me.

11 Pilates, he's still trying to weasel his way out of it. He knows that the governor always pardons a criminal at Passover, it's a tradition there in Jerusalem.

12 So he tells the priests, he says, "You have brought this man to me, as one that perverts the people: and, behold, I, having examined him before you, have found no fault in this man touching those things, whereof you accuse him. No, nor yet Herod: for I sent you to him; and lo, nothing worthy of death is done to him. I will therefore chastise him, and release him."

13 Now maybe I had some people in the crowd, and maybe I didn't. I sure as hell didn't give them any orders. But Herod, and Caiaphas, and maybe some big shots from Rome, maybe they have their people in the crowd, too.

14 Well, the crowd starts screaming, "Kill him! Crucify him!" And they all get together and chant, "Hang him up! Hang him up! Hang him up!" Crowds can get bloodthirsty, they go wild, I've seen it. But Pilates, he's not giving in. He says, "Why, what evil has he done? I have found no cause of death in him: I will therefore chastise him and let him go." The crowd keeps it up, "Hang him up! Hang him up! Hang him up!"

15 There was this other guy, Barabbas, he was supposed to be crucified that day, too. He was a thief and a murderer, and I hear he was plotting against the Romans on top of it, that's what people were telling me. The crowd starts yelling, "Give us Barabbas! We want Barabbas!"

16 Pilates says to the priests, he says, "Behold your King! Shall I crucify your King?" And the priests, they say, "We have no king but Caesar." Maybe the Romans paid off the priests, maybe they didn't. I had nothing to do with that, either, let me tell you, you can't believe what the fake scribes say. So the crowd, it gets Barabbas, he's set free, but Jesus, he's in a world of hurt.

17 Pilates, he takes a bowl of water, and he washes his hands. He says, "I am innocent of the blood of this just person." I heard later that he thought the priests and Pharisees just wanted Jesus dead because they were envious, and that his wife was soft and didn't want him killed.

18 You have to be tough to be a governor, who cares what your wife thinks. And sometimes, you have to have someone killed. Maybe Pilates wasn't tough enough, he wasn't tough like me. So Pilates takes this little whip—it was tiny, like a little sex toy he got from his wife or something—and he whips Jesus, but gently, not like it should've been done.

19 Then they take him into a hall, and some soldiers take off his purple robe, and they put that dirty white robe back on him, the same piece of crap he was wearing when I first saw him at the Jordan River with John. They weave a fake little crown out of thorns and put it on his head, and they put a reed into his hand like a scepter, and they bow down and call him "King of the Jews," laughing and spitting on him the whole time.

20 Then they scourge him, but good this time, with a real whip, crack! crack! crack! until he's bleeding all over. And they haul him out to the street, and they have a cross down there. Maybe his dad Joseph made it, I don't know, but wouldn't that be funny!

21 And they make him carry this cross through town, block after block, but he's too weak. Not like me, I could've carried that thing for miles. But Jesus, he's falling down all over the place trying to carry this thing, and there are hundreds of people, maybe more, following along.

22 And there's this dark-skinned guy, a hillbilly named Simon—not Simon Peter, or the other apostle Simon, it was another Simon, the third one for crying out loud—and they make him carry it the rest of the way.

23 They go up to this little hill called Golgotha, it's named after a skull, and they lay the cross on the ground with two other crosses, one on each side. They had two other losers to crucify that day, it was a threefer.

24 The soldiers, just for fun, they give Jesus a cup of vinegar to drink, but he spits it out. Then they nail his hands and feet to the cross, and Jesus, he's

crying and moaning the whole time, the little wimp. I have bone spurs in my feet, that's why I couldn't fight with my dad back in Gaul—it's true, the fake scribes don't know what they're talking about—but do you hear me crying and moaning? No way.

25 Then they hoist up the crosses, one at a time, and on the top of Jesus's cross they've hung a sign, "Jesus of Nazareth, King of the Jews." That was a nice touch, it went well with the crown of thorns.

26 So there's Jesus, and the two other losers, they were both thieves, one on each side. There they are, three bigtime losers, out there roasting in the sun. Someone, and it wasn't me, some comedian says, "Hey, look on the bright side!" And he starts whistling, and a bunch of people start whistling right along. You have to admit, that was pretty funny.

27 One of these thieves goes to razzing Jesus, he says, "Hey, why don't you get us down from here, huh?" But the other, he says, "Do you not fear God, seeing you are in the same condemnation? And we indeed justly; for we receive the due reward of our deeds: but this man has done nothing wrong."

28 And Jesus, he says to this second loser, **Truly I say to you, Today you shall be with me in paradise.** Yeah, right, that forever condo in heaven thing. I'll give him credit, he's playing out the eternal life scam until the very end.

29 There are a lot of people watching, and this one joker, he says, "You that destroy the Temple, and build it in three days, Save yourself, and come down from the cross." The temple priests, they're razzing Jesus, too, saying, "He saved others; himself he cannot save. Let Christ the King of Israel descend now from the cross, that we may see and believe."

30 Little Jesus, he thought he was so high and mighty, maybe he deserved to be brought down a peg. He sure had shut the hell up, this guy with the big mouth! All he says back is, **Father, forgive them; they know not what they do.** Weak, very weak.

31 So he hangs out for a while, and it starts to get boring. Crucifixion, it's not good entertainment, like a beheading. So the crowd starts to head on home,

except for the soldiers, and some of Jesus's friends—you know, the ones that didn't run away like scared rabbits.

32 His mother is there, the Vermin Mary, and another lady named Mary Magdalene. I heard she was a whore, that's what people told me, not bad looking, not bad at all. And another Mary, Mary of Clopas, she was there, what an ugly woman she was, a real pig, a real dog.

33 There were mostly women there, the men didn't have the stones to stick around. I'll give them credit, I have great respect for women, nobody has more respect for women than I do, even the disgusting ones and the ugly ones and the whores.

34 It was a weird afternoon, it was real dark for some reason, for, like, three hours. Probably a sandstorm, I don't know.

35 Then Jesus, he cries out, **Eli, Eli, lama sabachthani?** That's the best he could come up with? Where was his scriptwriter? Talk about your dopey famous last words, it was gibberish!

36 Later some people told me he was quoting the Torah in his own language, and that he was saying that his death was predicted by the prophets. They told me some Jew King, King David, wrote it, and that these Jew prophets, Moses and Elijah and Isaiah, knew it was Jesus who'd come be their savior and King of the Jews.

37 What a bunch of hogwash! Messiah, my ass, there's no such thing. He was one helluva magician, though, I can tell you that.

38 Well, it was getting late, and the soldiers were getting antsy. Jesus looks down, and he says, **I thirst.** His friends, they want to give him some water, but this one guy, he takes a sponge and gives him more vinegar instead.

39 I could tell Jesus didn't have much left in him, hanging up there, the high and mighty Son of God and King of the Jews. High, yes, but mighty? Nope, not anymore.

40 Finally, and I do mean finally, he says, **It is finished. Father, into your hands I commend my spirit.** Then he lets out a long groan, and he gives up

the ghost. Kicks the bucket. Bites the dust. Buys the farm. Takes the dirt nap. Goes room temperature. You get the picture.

41 He was dead, dead as a doornail, as far as I could tell. One of the soldiers goes up to him and takes his spear, and he sticks it right in his side, just to make sure. A bunch of blood and water comes gushing out, so everyone figures, there's no doubt—the guy is d, e, a, d, dead.

42 I say to myself, I say, "Donald, that's the end of that." And I go to find Peter, or any of the apostles—except Judas, of course, the loser—to offer them a contract. And I figure, what the hell, I offered Jesus a hundred million, I'll offer these jerks a hundred thousand, and they'll take it in a second. A magic act is a magic act, after all, and whoever I hire, they can use Jesus's name all they want to now.

43 So they take Jesus down off the cross, and the Vermin Mary, and these two other Marys, and a bunch of people who'd been following Jesus ever since he started in Galilee, they all want the body.

44 There was this rich guy—not as rich as me, I was worth fifteen, maybe eighteen billion sesterces—there was this rich guy named Joseph. Not Low Energy Joseph, the sissy, who was the Vermin Mary's husband, it's another Joseph, he was from Arimathea. Three Simons, four Marys, two Jameses, two Josephs—these people need to think up a few more names, it's ridiculous.

45 Anyway, Joseph goes to Pompous Pilates, and he asks for the body. He doesn't want the Jews to get it, who knows what they would have done with it. Pilates, he asks a centurion, is Jesus really dead? And the centurion, he says, "Sure enough, we stuck him like a pig, and he didn't flinch."

46 But this other centurion, he must've been scammed but good by Jesus, because he says, "Truly this was the Son of God." So maybe Jesus had a centurion on the inside after all, I don't know.

47 Joseph takes the body, and these women from Galilee, including who knows how many Marys, they oil it up real good, and they throw in a bunch of spices, to keep down the smell, you know. Then they wrap it up in sheets, and they put a napkin around its head.

48 And right near where the crucifixion was, there's a little cave carved into the stone, in a little garden there. So they put the body in the little cave, and they roll a big stone in front of it, like they did with Lazarus. But they don't have a funeral or anything, because it's their little Sabbath day, so they have to wait.

49 Now the temple priests and the Pharisees, they're worried the apostles will try to steal the body. They tell Pilates, "Sir, we remember that the deceiver said, while he was yet alive, After three days I will rise again. Command therefore that the sepulcher be made sure until the third day, lest his disciples come by night, and steal him away, and say to the people, He is risen from the dead."

50 Pilates says, "You may have a watch: go your way, make it as sure as you can." So they go and seal the stone into the cave, and they get some watchmen to guard it.

51 I can tell you, because I was there, that Jesus sure looked dead, and that he was put in that cave. And I know the temple priests and Pharisees sealed the cave, I saw it myself. And I know they kept a watch on it, because I had *my* people watching, too.

52 So I was finished with Jesus, he had his chance, but he blew it. When I'm finished with someone, that's it, I'm done with them for good. I don't give anybody a second chance, no way.

53 I wanted to stay in Jerusalem for a few days and take care of business. I'd had enough with these lunatics, the apostles and the Marys and all those sheep from Galilee. I had my people keep an eye on Peter and the other apostles, though, I still wanted to hire them to do shows in my properties.

54 The Jew Sabbath comes and goes, and this is where it gets weird, I mean, really weird. So the Sabbath ends, and the week begins, and two of the Marys go back to the cave. But the stone has been moved away from the cave, and there's no Jesus in there!

55 One of my guys, he comes and gets me, and I hustle over to the cave. A bunch of people are running the same way I am, to the cave, and some are running from the cave back into town. It's chaos, totally out of control.

56 I get to the cave, and there's Mary Magdalene, and Aint Peter, and two or three apostles—one was this young guy, John, he was the youngest apostle, he looked like a little girl—all freaking out and talking at the same time. I can hardly figure out what the hell is going on.

57 Mary, she swears that an angel came down from heaven and rolled the stone away, and told her to run get the apostles, and that's why Peter and John are there. Peter and John, they both peek into the cave, and they say they see the linens and the napkin, but no Jesus. One guy says that when he got there, there were two angels in the cave, dressed in white. Another says there was just a young kid there.

58 For years after, people were talking about that day, and they never did get their stories straight. I even heard there was an earthquake right before the stone rolled away, but I didn't feel anything. It was all a hoax as far as I'm concerned, a total hoax. All I know is that half the Jews in Judea wrote stories about Jesus, and they all say something different about that day.

59 Anyway, back to the story. They're all wondering, where the hell is Jesus? And they all head off in different directions, who knows what they were looking for.

60 I stay there with a Mary, it was Mary Magdalene, the whore, and we peek into the cave. The linen and the napkin are still there, like Jesus had just taken them off and walked away. And these two guys are standing there, one where Jesus's head would have been and one at the feet, and sure enough, they're wearing white.

61 I figure, here's all the proof I need. These guys have taken the body away, and now they're cleaning up the scene of the crime. One of them says, "Woman, why do you weep?" And Mary Magdalene says, "Because they have taken away my Lord, and I know not where they have laid him."

62 So she turns around to leave, and so do I, and what do you think we see? Jesus! He's standing right there! I about had a cow, let me tell you. It was Jesus, or I'm not Donald of Gaul.

63 But Mary, she doesn't recognize him, I guess she was in shock. Jesus, he says, **Woman, why do you weep? Whom do you seek?** And she thinks he's the gardener or something, and she says, "Sir, if you have borne him from here, tell me where you have laid him, and I will take him away."

64 Then Jesus says, **Mary.** And all of a sudden, she recognizes him, and she says, "Master!" And Jesus, he says, **Touch me not; for I am not yet ascended to my Father: but go to my brothers and sisters, and say to them, I ascend to my Father, and your Father; and to my God, and your God.**

65 Now Jesus, he's totally ignoring me. And I'm not stupid, I'm trying to figure out what the hell just happened. Maybe there were twins, like, identical twins, who knows. That's all I can think of. Maybe the Vermin Mary had twins with that Crooked Gabriel, and back in Bethlehem, they put one in the manger in the barn, and the other was in the hotel in Bethlehem, where he belonged.

66 Maybe they weren't going to fake a crucifixion, they were going to have a real one! And then, with one twin gone—boy, you wouldn't want to draw the short straw on that one—with one twin gone, the other would come out of hiding and pretend to be Jesus, back from the dead.

67 Or maybe, someone high up was in on it, like Pompous Pilates, or Herod Antipasto. Or they paid off the centurions and soldiers who did the crucifixion. Who knows, they pulled it off one way or another. However they did it, what a magic trick! The best ever!

68 And what a scam! I'll bet they'd already collected millions, probably billions, of sesterces. And this way, they could keep it all, every quadrans, and no one would ask for a refund. The marks, they'd all be waiting to die themselves, then go get that condo in heaven and be with Jesus.

69 So Mary, and Peter, and John, and all the apostles except Judas and Thomas, they meet back at the house where I catered their last supper. And I'm hiding behind the curtain—remember, there was a curtain there—so I see the whole thing. They were afraid the Jews would come and get them, and the last thing they needed was to get crucified themselves, or for Jesus to get crucified twice. Once is enough for anyone.

70 Then Jesus walks in, or his twin, who knows. I started calling him Jeff, anyway, short for "Jesus Effing Christ." And Jeff, he says, **Peace be with you.** But the apostles, they're sitting there with stupid looks on their faces. I mean, who'd believe a man could come back from the dead?

71 Jeff, he sees what's going on, so he holds out his hands, and holds up his feet, and pulls up his robe. And would you believe it, there are holes in his hands, and holes in his feet, and a big fat gash in his side, just where the Roman soldier had stuck him three days before.

72 Jeff, he says, **As my Father has sent me, even so send I you. Receive the Holy Ghost: Whose sins you remit, they are remitted to them; and whose sins you retain, they are retained.**

73 So the scam lives on, only now, they have this whole resurrection angle. Talk about branding and promoting, they can tell everyone their "savior" came back from the dead! Think how much easier it would be to bilk a sucker out of his life savings with that sham, it would be easy as pie, believe me.

74 By now, I thought I'd seen everything. But along comes Thomas, and he says, "Except I shall see in his hands the print of the nails, and put my finger into the print of the nails, and thrust my hand into his side, I will not believe."

75 Finally, I say to myself, finally someone with some brains. But here's how far Gabriel and Jeff would go for the scam. Jeff, he says, **Reach here your finger, Thomas, and behold my hands; and reach here your hand, and thrust it into my side: and be not faithless, but believing.**

76 Well that's exactly what Thomas does, and believe it or not, there were actual holes in Jeff's hands, and a real honest to God gash in his side. Thomas, his eyes get big, and he bows down and says to Jeff, "My Lord and my God."

77 Jeff says, **Thomas, because you have seen me, you have believed: blessed are they that have not seen, and yet have believed.**

78 Truer words were never spoken. Blessed indeed are all the losers who didn't see any of this, but still believe it, bless their little hearts. Somewhere,

Gabriel must have been laughing his head off at those suckers, laughing all the way to the bank.

79 Then Jeff says, **Tis more blessed to give, than to receive.** I say to myself, "Like hell it is, you've got that backwards." But what a sales pitch when you're trying to get someone to sell everything they have and give every penny to you.

80 Like I said before, any good performer knows, you have to go out on a high note. I could tell Jeff was just about done with these shills of his, he didn't need to waste his time with them anymore, and it was time to go back to Gabriel and split the loot.

81 So he stands up, and he says, **These are the words which I spoke to you, while I was yet with you, that all the things must be fulfilled, which were written in the law of Moses, and in the prophets, and in the psalms, concerning me.**

82 **Thus it is written, and thus it behooved Christ to suffer, and to rise from the dead the third day. All power is given to me in heaven and on earth.**

83 **Go therefore into all the world, and preach the gospel to every creature in all nations, baptizing them in the name of the Father, and of the Son, and of the Holy Ghost: teaching them to observe all things I have commanded you.**

84 **He that believes and is baptized shall be saved: but he that believes not shall be damned. And repentance and remission of sins should be preached in my name among all nations, beginning in Jerusalem.**

85 Not bad, not bad at all. The whole scam in a nutshell, heaven, hell, the works. And he was expanding their sales territory, sending them all over, to "all nations, beginning in Jerusalem." But he wasn't through just yet, not Jesus, he had one more trick up his sleeve, and it was a doozy.

86 I don't know how he did it, but it took some doing, okay? He steps outside, and he smiles that sad smile of his one last time, and then he looks up— and he just floats away into the sky! I mean, he literally floats up into the sky!

87 He's holding his arms out, and his knees are bent just a little, and his filthy robe is bright white all of a sudden, and up he floats, up up and away, until he disappears into a cloud!

88 There must have been mirrors, maybe balloons, a mannequin, maybe a crane somewhere out of sight. I don't know how they did it, but I know what I saw. What a finish, what a finale. It was fantastic, absolutely fantastic, the best magic trick ever. I could hardly believe my eyes.

89 Now you can just imagine what these apostles must have been thinking. I guess they thought that Jesus was up in heaven, getting their condos ready. They went out from then on, preaching up a storm about Jesus, or Jeff, or whatever you want to call him, and bilking people all over the empire.

90 Jesus, or Jeff, was seen a few times after that, first in a little backwater called Emmaus, and then over by the Sea of Galilee. All kinds of fakers claim to have seen him over the years, they see him walking down the street, they see him in the sky, they see him in a bowl of spaghetti, it's nuts.

91 Gabriel and Jesus, or Jeff, they must be somewhere right now—maybe in the Orient, who knows, but that's where I think they are—they must be somewhere, laughing it up and enjoying their mansions and their money, probably with the Vermin Mary and whoever else is in on the scam.

92 I guess I'll never know. But that's not quite the end of the story. The scam wasn't over, not by a long shot. *This* scam had legs, let me tell you, it wasn't going anywhere anytime soon.

93 In fact, it went on for more than three more decades.

12 It was time to get back to Rome and back to business. I'm in the hospitality business, and all my inns and taverns, all my bathhouses and casinos and theaters, they weren't going to run themselves.

2 And twenty billion sesterces, you know everyone wants a piece of that! I was the richest man in Rome, after the emperor, of course. Praise Be to Caesar, that's what I always say. You have to kiss his ring, if you know what I mean.

3 I'd wasted two, almost three years on this guy, Jesus. I kept some people over in Judea looking for him, or for his twin, Jeff—I never figured that out, nobody did—looking for him, or them, and for Gabriel. And some of my other people, they kept an eye on the apostles, but I never could sign any of them to a contract.

4 On the bright side, all that time in Judea wasn't wasted. I built a pretty good business over there, headquartered in Jerusalem, and I recruited a lot of talent over there—some gorgeous dancing girls, and some of the best business talent I've ever hired. The Jews, you've got to love them, they're incredible businessmen.

5 Kohn and Kohen, my lawyers in Rome, they were Jews, like I said before, great lawyers, really terrific. I hired them before I ever went to Judea. They were the best, even if they came to bad ends.

6 Kohn, he got disbarred by the Romans, he took things a little too far with a Senator and worked for one too many gangsters, and then he died from a social disease. And Kohen, he got busted by the Romans and disbarred, too, and thrown into prison. I had nothing to do with that, he wasn't working for me at the time, no matter what he says, no matter what the fake scribes say. You can't trust those people, they're terrible.

7 As everyone knows, Emperor Tiberius had kicked all the Jews out of Rome back when I first got there, about ten years before I met John and Jesus. And Emperor Claudius kicked them out again about twenty years after Jesus was crucified, when I was back in Rome. I was allowed to keep my Jews around both times, though, because I'm rich, and I know who to pay off.

8 If it was up to me, I'd keep all the useful immigrants around to do whatever they do best, and kick the rest right back to wherever they belong. Africa, Arabia, wherever. Maybe ban them from coming to Rome, maybe build a wall.

Whatever, you have to keep the undesirables out, or things will get out of control, totally out of control.

9 If it was up to me, I'd keep all the homeless and the refugees and the beggars out of sight somewhere, too. You can't have them stinking up the place, you have to keep the markets and the Forum clean and looking good. Put them in pens, like cattle, that's what I'd do, and keep the poor in their ghettos while I'm at it, and don't let them out.

10 That's not what the apostles would do, though, not by a long shot. Jesus, he always said to coddle the poor, "the least of these my brothers and sisters," like they were special or something. You know, feed the hungry, give water to the thirsty, clothe the naked, all that crazy talk.

11 What a bunch of goody two shoes. It's businessmen like me who make the empire run, not those losers. People who can't take care of themselves, that's their problem, not mine. If you give them something for nothing, you'll just have more of them, and who wants that? Sharing, it's weak, if you ask me.

12 In fact, and it'll get me back to the story, the apostles, and all the losers who started following them—they called themselves "Christians"—they wanted to share *everything*. I mean, share *every single thing*. Share it equally, no matter how hard someone like me worked for it, or no matter if some bum didn't work at all.

13 These Christians, after they'd been suckered into the scam, they shared everything they had, nobody owned anything! They held everything in common. They were *commonists*, that's what they were. They were dangerous, very danger-ous, they could pull down the whole empire with that kind of nonsense.

14 One, his name was Paul, he even said, "The love of money is the root of all evil: which while some coveted after, they have erred from the faith, and pierced themselves through with many sorrows.

15 "O man of God, flee from these things: and follow after righteousness, godliness, faith, love, patience, meekness. Charge them that are rich in this world, that they be not high minded, nor trust in uncertain riches, but in the

living God, who gives us richly all things to enjoy; That they do good, that they be rich in good works, ready to distribute, willing to communicate."

16 Can you imagine? Share everything, distribute your riches? What kind of world would that be? And why shouldn't I be high minded, I'm better than all those losers, I'm better than anyone, except Caesar, of course. And who the hell wants to be meek, or patient? That's for losers, not winners like me. I win all the time, win, win, win.

17 Paul, what a moron, I'd like to punch him in the face. They call him Paul the Apostle, but I call him Paul the Apostate. (That one's not mine, one of my secretaries came up with it, it means he's a traitor, okay?)

18 Let me tell you, this Jesus, he put a lot of bad ideas out there, and his apostles, they wanted to spread them all over the empire and beyond. They didn't believe that crap themselves, they didn't believe one word of it. It was just a way to get people to give them everything they owned. What a scam, a total hoax, it was pathetic.

19 Paul the Apostate, he was a loser, a real loser. He didn't come around until a few years after Jesus was crucified, but him and Peter, they took these crazy ideas and spread them all over, for more than thirty years if you can believe it. The scam just wouldn't die.

20 Over those thirty-something years, Paul wrote letters to half the people in the Roman Empire, in Greek, the moron, and he had them copied for the whole world to see. I've had some of them translated myself, I'll get to that at the end.

21 I think if they could, Peter, Paul, and Mary—what a trio—they would have brought down Rome, just to keep this scam going! Nothing can bring down Rome, though, that's why I got out of Gaul and came here. Wealth is wealth, and power is power, and that's all that matters. (A little fame, that's alright, too.)

22 Like I said, back to the story, which I got from some of my best people. Right after Jesus supposedly came back from the dead, and magically rose up to heaven, the apostles met again in Jerusalem. Supposedly, Jesus popped down

again and told them to stay in Jerusalem, until he was ready for them to pick up where they left off.

23 He said, **John truly baptized with water; but you shall be baptized with the Holy Ghost not many days from now. You shall receive power, after that the Holy Ghost is come upon you: and you shall be witnesses for me both in Jerusalem, and in all Judea, and in Samaria, and into the uttermost parts of the world.**

24 It was another sales talk, a pep talk. He was going to send these apostles all over the world to open sales offices. They called them "churches," but they were really just sales offices, just franchises, that's what they were, believe me.

25 By Jupiter, how much money could they make with these franchises spreading all over the place? I mean, all over the empire, and beyond? Billions and billions, tens of billions, hundreds of billions, who knows?

26 So later, they met again, these apostles, and this time Aint Peter stood up and made himself Chief Executive Officer of the business. There were, like, 120 people there, so they'd been franchising in the meantime, a classic pyramid scheme as far as I can tell. The Vermin Mary was there, and a bunch of other women, mostly from Galilee.

27 Well, Judas was gone, maybe dead, and the organizational chart had twelve positions, so they had to replace him. They had two candidates, another guy named Joseph (Jeez, that's three) and a guy named Matthias. They did this job interview thing, sort of like the reality theater idea I pitched to Jesus when he chose the first twelve apostles.

28 They picked Matthias, and on one of their Jew feast days—they call it Pentecost, it was fifty days after Passover—they had another business meeting. And supposedly, a big wind came into the room they were in, blowing stuff all over the place, and then shazam! Little tongues of fire started licking them.

29 Yeah, I know, that's a weird magic trick, but what do you expect from these people? They'll believe anything, as long as you throw in a little magic. It's pathetic what they'll believe, totally pathetic.

30 Then they started talking in all kinds of different languages, not just in Hebrew or Aramaic, like usual. There were Jews from all over the world in Jerusalem, and no matter where they were from, they could understand these apostles. And I mean they were from everywhere, Greece, Mesopotamia, Asia, Egypt, Ethiopia, Arabia, you name it.

31 The apostles, they pretended that it was magic, that God gave them the gift to be understood in any language. I figure, Jesus and Gabriel made them learn all those languages so the scam could spread as far as possible, you know, to maximize profits. What an idea, I wish I'd thought of it.

32 Aint Peter, he started preaching again, now that he was CEO. He said, "You men of Israel, hear these words: Jesus of Nazareth, a man approved of God among you by miracles and wonders and signs. Him you have crucified and slain; whom God has raised up, having loosed the pains of death.

33 "For David spoke concerning him, being a prophet, he seeing this before spoke of the resurrection of Christ. This Jesus has God raised up, whereof we are all witnesses. Therefore let all the house of Israel know assuredly, that God has made that same Jesus, whom you have crucified, both Lord and Christ."

34 Well, Aint Peter, he went on and on, and before you know it, there were, like, 3000 of these Christians, all of them believing Jesus was the Son of God— you know, NoWay—and all of them ready to spread the scam around the world.

35 Where the hell did they find these people? They were nuts, they gave up all their possessions, and they held everything in common—like I said, they were commonists!

36 But let me tell you something, no one is really a commonist, everybody loves money, everybody. And all that loot, most of it was going right back to Gabriel and Jesus. And Peter, Paul, and Mary, and all the apostles—apostles, my ass, they were salesmen—you can bet they were getting their cuts of the loot, too.

37 One place that loot wasn't going, was into the hands of the temple priests and Pharisees. So they took Peter, and they took John, and they locked them up and told them to shut the hell up about Jesus. But by then, there were, like, 5000 of these Christians! Talk about multi-level marketing, these guys were good!

38 The next day, Caiaphas, and the elders and scribes and temple priests, they all got together and asked Peter who the hell he thought he was. He said, "Be it known to you all, and to all the people of Israel, that by the name of Jesus Christ of Nazareth, whom you crucified, whom God raised from the dead, even by him does this man stand here before you whole."

39 A little while later, Caiaphas and the others, they told Peter and the apostles to shut the hell up again, *or else*, but there were just too many Christians by then, the whole thing was out of control.

40 These Christians, they were loyal, I'll give them that. Every one of them shared or sold everything they had—exactly what Jesus tried to make *me* do—and took all the goods and the money and laid it at the feet of the apostles. All but this one guy, Ananias was his name, he wouldn't do it.

41 Ananias, he sold his land, but he kept back some of the money. When he only laid part of the money at Peter's feet, Peter said, "Why has Satan filled your heart to lie to the Holy Ghost, and to keep back part of the price of the land?"

42 Ananias, he fell down and died right there, at least that's what the Christians say, but don't you believe it. They had this guy whacked for holding out, that's how a protection racket works. You have to be ruthless, you have to scare the crap out of people, that's how it works.

43 Then his wife came to Peter, she didn't know Ananias was dead yet. And Peter said, "Tell me whether you sold the land for so much? How is it that you have agreed together to tempt the Spirit of the Lord?" Then she fell down and died right there, too, probably with a knife in her back, if you ask me.

44 So this story gets around, and you'd better believe, after that, nobody's holding out. Every Christian's giving every quadrans and denarius to the apostles. And for what? A promise that when they die, they'll go to heaven and get it all back times a hundred. The idiots, they didn't deserve any better.

45 But people start coming from all around, and the apostles are doing their magic tricks again, healing the sick left and right, casting out demons, raising the dead, the whole shebang. Sales offices are opening up like crazy, and the whole thing just starts rolling along like a snowball. It was crazy, totally crazy.

46 The temple priests tried one more time to get rid of these guys. They locked up all the apostles in Jerusalem, but overnight, the apostles broke out of the prison. They said angels let them out, but I know better. They bribed the guards, that's how they got out. Money talks, everyone knows that, you can bribe anyone, and I should know.

47 So the priests had the apostles beaten, and they told them once and for all to shut the hell up about Jesus. But there were so many of these Christians by then, that who knows what would have happened if they started locking them all up, or killing them all, and that's what it would have taken, that I can tell you.

48 By then, the apostles, they were tired of doing the bookkeeping and all the grunt work, and being threatened and thrown in jail and beaten. So they chose seven deacons, sort of mid-level management, to stay in Jerusalem and run the business—and take the heat, see—while they went out and traveled. Not a bad idea, not bad at all.

49 One of the deacons was named Stephen, he was their leader, he was like Peter and Jesus—he could preach up a storm. He ran the whole Jerusalem office, the headquarters. Peter, he took off for Samaria and Greece, he lived in Antioch and Corinth, and he wound up in Rome, but I'll get to that soon enough.

50 Stephen got too big for his britches, and Jews from all over were getting worried about these Christians, so they decided to take him down. They brought a bunch of muscle to Jerusalem, and they told Stephen one last time to shut the hell up about Jesus, or else. Only now, he didn't have Peter or the apostles to back him up.

51 Stephen, he didn't give in, he preached every day about the history of the Jews, and he said that Jesus was the messiah, and all the Jews should follow him from then on. That was a mistake, a big mistake, because they hauled Stephen out of town, and what did they do? They stoned him to death, that's what!

52 I figure, that's how you handle these people, if they won't listen to reason, you have to take them out, permanently. You have to be tough, that's what my father taught me, and that's what Kohn taught me. Stephen, he learned it the hard way, he got his skull busted open like a melon.

53 Then there was Paul the Apostate, he was the worst of them, a real turn-coat. He was a Jew—a Pharisee, actually—and a Roman, and at first, he didn't like these Christians at all. He was from Tarsus, in Cilicia. Paul was there when Stephen was stoned, and he was all for it, maybe he threw the first rock, who knows.

54 In fact, Paul had thousands of Christians rounded up and put in prison, and he had some of them whacked. That's what the Jews and the Romans should have done from the first, but they didn't have the guts.

55 After Stephen was stoned to death, Paul headed over to Damascus, in the Kingdom of Aram. He was going to bring a whole mess of Christians to Jerusalem to be punished. Just outside of Damascus, Paul, he keeled over, and as far as I can tell, he must've hit his head, and I mean, hit it hard.

56 According to Paul, a bright light shined down from the sky, and a voice came down, and it said, **Saul, Saul, why do you persecute me? I am Jesus of Nazareth, whom you persecute. Arise, and go into Damascus; and there it shall be told all things which are appointed for you to do.**

57 Saul, that's the Jew name for Paul—jeez, can these people just get their names right? Anyway, Paul was blinded by the light, but from then on, he believed in Jesus, too. Another sheep, baa, baa, baa, that's what I say. He was blind for three days, that's what he said, but I think he was blind from then on, if you know what I mean.

58 So he went back to Jerusalem to pray in the temple, and he supposedly heard Jesus talking to him again. This time, Jesus said, **Make haste, and get quickly out of Jerusalem: for they will not receive your testimony concerning me. Depart: for I will send you far away among the Gentiles.**

59 The gentiles! Boy did that open up the market! Remember, at first Jesus told them to market to the Jews, not the Gentiles. Not a bad idea, start with your best demographic, then expand. So maybe he had some business sense after all, maybe he wasn't as dense as I thought he was.

60 Then Paul the Apostate went all over the place, and I do mean all over the place, for decades, preaching about Jesus. Arabia, Greece, Cyprus, Asia,

Macedonia, Anatolia, Rhodes, Hispania, you name it, he went there. He even went to Caesarea Maritima, where this whole story began.

61 And he wrote letters to cities all over the place—Corinth, Galatia, Philippi, Ephesus, Thessalonica, Colossae, and, if you can believe it, Rome—telling people what to think about Jesus. The nerve of this guy, he wrote to us in Rome, like we gave a rat's ass what he thinks. What a clown.

62 It was Peter and Paul who took the scam worldwide. They must have been in touch with Crooked Gabriel and Jesus the whole time, and sending some loot wherever those mansions of theirs were.

63 Finally, these priests and Pharisees and some Greeks got hold of Paul, and they were going to kill him, but some Roman centurions saved him and threw him into prison. But nobody knew what to do with him, because for one, he was a Roman, and for another, he was a Pharisee. Plus, he was famous. You couldn't just kill him, there would have been hell to pay.

64 Sitting there in prison, he heard Jesus again. Jesus said, **Be of good cheer, Paul: for as you have testified of me in Jerusalem, so must you bear witness also at Rome.**

65 Sure, going to Rome, that sounds crazy, but this whole Christian thing was crazy, right? They bounced Paul around for a while, I mean, for several years, and he wound up on Malta, and then he finally got to Rome about thirty years after Jesus was crucified. And they put him under house arrest.

66 Well, guess who shows up in Rome about that same time? Aint Peter, that's who. These two guys, Peter and Paul, they'd spent thirty years running all over the Roman Empire scamming people into becoming Christians. The rest of the apostles, I lost track of them, but don't you know they were doing the same thing, and cleaning up.

67 So now these Christians were preaching all over Rome, speaking wherever they could find an audience. You know what, I wanted to hit a couple of those speakers so hard. I was gonna hit one guy in particular, a very little guy, I was gonna hit this guy so hard his head would spin. He wouldn't know what the hell happened. But I let him off the hook.

68 One of my secretaries even fell for the scam, she turned into a Christian. What a disgrace. So I told her boss, I said, "Get rid of her, get her out tomorrow. I don't care, get her out tomorrow. Take her out, okay? Do it." And guess what, he did it, he fired her, and pronto. No one says no to Donald of Gaul, no one.

69 And a security guy of mine, he fell for it, too, he became a Christian. So I fired him, too. And he had a twin brother, so I fired the twin, just for the hell of it. "You're fired," what beautiful words, I can't get enough of saying them, it's terrific. "You're fired, fired, fired."

70 By then, there were hundreds of Christian sales offices—these so-called "churches"—all over the empire, into Asia in the east, and all the way to Hispania in the west, and up into Gaul and Germania in the north, and down to Egypt and Carthage in the south. They were all over the place, like, everywhere.

71 There were tens of thousands of Christians, maybe hundreds of thousands, in practically every backwater town in every shithole country in the empire and beyond. It was crazy, unbelievable.

72 Can you imagine, all these thousands of people believing Jesus was the Son of God, and giving up all their possessions? Think what that could have done to the economy of the empire if it had spread too far! Think what it could have done to me, Donald of Gaul, if people stopped going to casinos and bath houses, and stopped hiring massage girls and watching wet tunic contests!

73 The Romans, they weren't stupid. They saw what was going on. These Christians, they put Jesus above Caesar. They let women have all kinds of power. They followed their own laws instead of the Romans'. They didn't believe in the pagan gods, and when pagan gods get mad, bad things happen.

74 Aside from the Jews and Christians, most everyone in the empire was a pagan. They had more gods than they knew what to do with, and you could worship whichever gods you wanted to. There were temples all over the place to every god you could name, and festivals all year round, it was fabulous.

75 The Jews had their one god, No Way, and the Christians, most of them were Jews like Jesus was, before the apostles got hold of them. So they still worshipped No Way, he still had that monopoly.

76 Now the pagans, they didn't like these Christians. A lot of what the Christians did, they did in secret, like the whole eating Jesus's flesh and drinking Jesus's blood thing. You have to admit, that's some weird stuff, just plain nuts. (And all because of a joke of mine about cannibals, can you believe it?)

77 When bad things happened, like floods and plagues, these pagans, they blamed the Christians for pissing off the pagan gods. That came in handy at the end, I'll get to that soon enough, too.

78 So a few nuts running around worshipping Jesus, you could put up with that, no problem. But after thirty-plus years of running the scam, there were enough Christians that the Romans, they were sick of it. And if I'm being perfectly honest, so was I, I'd had enough of them, more than enough.

79 Little Jesus, he turned down every offer I made him, over and over, he never let me in on the scam, not even for one lousy quadrans. Peter, he wouldn't even listen to me, and neither would any of the other apostles. No respect, I tell you, I got no respect from those people.

80 But guess who did respect me? The Roman authorities, that's who. I knew every consul and praetor and senator, and they knew me. I gave every last one of them plenty of money, and I had them treated like kings at all my properties, and I threw the best parties and invited every last one of them, that's what I did, and it worked.

81 That's how you get things done, that's how you get rich, you pay off all the politicians, and bigly, I mean, really bigly. Like I said before, if you can't get rich dealing with politicians, you've got a problem.

82 I even knew the emperors. Now, you can't pay off an emperor, he has more money than Jupiter. But I knew the emperors, too, and if I couldn't pay them off with cash, there were other ways to get what I wanted, if you know what I mean.

83 More than thirty years this scam had been running, and now Peter and Paul were in Rome, in the heart of the empire.

84 Something had to give.

13 This story of Little Jesus, let me wrap it up. By the time I decided to write this, there were hundreds of thousands of Christians, the idiots, worshipping Jesus and giving all their money to him and his gang. Weak people, very weak.

2 The apostles, probably hundreds of them by now, they were cashing in big time. I'm sure they took their cut, plus a little extra. And as if that wasn't enough, some of them started to write scrolls about Jesus and make a little extra that way. I'd written some scrolls myself, and they made me a bundle, believe me. So I wrote this story of Jesus, and it's going to make me even richer than I already am.

3 Anything I write, it sells big time, because I'm the richest man in Rome, and I'm the most famous, after the emperor, of course. Everything I touch, it turns to gold. And don't believe the fake scribes when they say I have ghost writers do the work. I have the best words, my words are the best, I write it all by myself.

4 I don't get any respect, though, no one gives me credit. I'm worth twenty, maybe twenty-five billion sesterces now. I've been a praetor, and a consul, and I could be a senator anytime I want, but it would be a big step down. I know how to get elected, I know how to use the system. I know how it's rigged. I could be anything I want, and I do mean, *anything*.

5 The elites hate me, they don't think I'm smart, just lucky. And they think I'm unfair, and unbalanced. Don't believe anything the fake scribes write, they work for the elites, and the elites hate me. It's a disgrace, a total disgrace.

6 I'm balanced, alright, throughout my life my two greatest assets have been mental stability and being, like, really smart. I went from *very* successful businessman, to top reality theater star, and if I wanted, I could probably run the whole Roman Empire. (I don't want that, of course, Praise Be to Caesar.)

7 I think that would qualify as not smart, but genius. And a very stable genius at that, I'm a stable genius, and anyone who doesn't think I'm stable is full of horse shit. I have one of the great temperaments, I have a winning temperament. I have a strong temperament, folks, I think I have a great temperament.

8 And look at me, I'm in my seventies, and I'm in perfect shape, like a gladiator. My physical strength and stamina, they're extraordinary. My health, it's astonishingly excellent, especially my mental health. If I was the emperor I'd be the healthiest individual ever selected to the emperorship. (Not that I want that, I'm just saying.)

9 Physical perfection is important to me, I surround myself with physical perfection, just look at my wives and secretaries. I mean, you should see me ride a horse, or one of my secretaries—they ride horses, too.

10 In fact, just to show the fake scribes what's what, I've instructed my longtime physician to issue a full medical report. It will show perfection, that's what it'll show. Not that I have anything to do with it, he's a physician, he's writing the report himself, you can trust me on that.

11 Anyway, it's been, like, thirty-two years since Jesus disappeared, and look at me, look at what I've done. All these Christians, they worship Jesus, they love him, but who worships me, Donald of Gaul? Who loves me like that? Nobody, that's who. It's not fair, it's totally unfair.

12 Jesus was captured, does being captured make you a hero? I don't think so, I think it makes you a loser. I like people who weren't captured, okay? I like people who weren't crucified. And where is Jesus now? Probably looking at me, Donald of Gaul, and turning over in his grave.

13 Plenty of people follow Donald of Gaul, don't get me wrong, they follow me like sheep. They just don't think I'm a god, or the son of a god, that's all. I have rallies all the time, you should see them. Thousands of people, tens of thousands, chanting my name and waving my banners. I can fill any arena, my crowds are the biggest.

14 Julius Caesar, Rome made him a god after he was assassinated by those weasels in the Senate. Augustus Caesar, Rome made him a god, too, he even had temples built for himself. Caligula, he was worshipped like a god, he even had a statue of himself put in the Temple in Jerusalem. But what about Donald of Gaul? Nothing. Jesus, they worship as a god, but not me? That's just not right.

15 Even when I was young, back in Avaricum, in Gaul, where I'm from, I didn't get any respect. I was rich, and I earned it. They said I got everything from my father, like, four hundred million sesterces' worth, but that's just not true.

16 My dad gave me a small loan, maybe a million sesterces, and yeah, maybe he helped me out when my first casino was in trouble. But I'm a self-made man, I earned everything I have on my own. People think I'm not as good as my dad, but they're wrong, I'm richer than he ever was. And my mother, she loved me, my mother loved me, don't believe what the fake scribes say about that.

17 The elites in Rome, they don't respect me, either. They think I'm a hill-billy because I'm from Gaul. But I'm richer than any of them, I'm very rich, I'm worth billions and billions, like, twenty-five or thirty billion sesterces. I have some of the best palaces in the empire, pretty soon maybe I'll have *the* best.

18 I throw the best dinners, too, no Trimalchio's dinner can hold a candle to mine. And you should see my tomb, it's better than any emperor's tomb, it's better than any Trimalchio's tomb. But I won't be needing it any time soon, unlike some people I know.

19 You don't mess with me, you don't mess with Donald of Gaul. Once, this little pipsqueak, his name was Timothy, he spread a rumor all over Rome that I wasn't worth even one billion sesterces. I sued him for all he was worth, I spent millions on it just to put him in his place. It cost him a fortune. That's what the courts are for, so great men like me can squash little rats like him.

20 What's the law to me, anyway? If you break the law a hundred times, you might get caught once, and if you get caught ten times, you might pay the price once, and when you finally do pay the price, you probably made a thousand times more than it cost you. Do the math. I've been in, like, four thousand lawsuits, and it's paid off, it's paid off bigly.

21 If you're rich like me, the law is a great thing, it's a tool. And the courts, they can be bought, they can be rigged, that's just the price of doing business. The law means nothing, the only thing that matters is winning.

22 Even the Senate can be bought, and what you can't get with money, you can get other ways. Like Kohn taught me, you can make the Senate do anything

you want it to do. If a Senator stands up to you, you squash him, and the others will come around, that's how it works.

23 I don't get it, why do so many people worship Jesus, what the hell did he do? Some magic tricks, and a clever little scheme to bilk people out of their life savings, that's what. Pathetic, totally pathetic.

24 Even the emperors, what did they do? All they had to do was be born, and bing bang bong, they were on top without lifting a finger. All except Julius Caesar, he earned it, he raised armies and took what he wanted, and he took that measly Roman Republic and made it his.

25 Republic, my ass. Who needs a damn republic? Who needs laws and elections, why the hell would you give any power to peasants, or merchants, or soldiers in the first place? You might as well have a damn democracy, like the Greeks, those idiots. You might as well let the peasants run the place, you might as well let them elect an African emperor.

26 Rome took Greece like taking candy from a baby, that's how weak democracy is. I'll tell you one thing, though, if Rome was a democracy, I'd be emperor myself. No one knows branding like I do, no one knows marketing, and that's the secret to democracy. You have to know how to market yourself to the peasants. And no one knows better than me how to manipulate the peasants, let me tell you.

27 First, you appeal to the strongest emotion: fear. You make people afraid, you make them afraid of being invaded, afraid of immigrants, afraid of Africans and Arabs, afraid of their own government, afraid of losing their money, afraid of commonists, afraid of taxes. Get them trembling in their boots. Jesus and the Christians, they did the same thing, only they used the fear of death, and the fear of hell, to run their scam.

28 Then you appeal to the second strongest emotion: greed. You offer them higher wages, lower taxes, a richer empire, a time of plenty. Get them drooling for more, more than they ever thought they could have. Tell them you'll stop sending money all over the empire, you'll keep it right here in Rome, and when you conquer a place, you'll take everything it's got and bring it all home.

29 Jesus and the Christians, they did that, too, they told their marks they'd get back their money a hundred times over. Only they tricked them into thinking they'd get their treasures in heaven, *after they died*, the suckers.

30 You have to have some scapegoats, too. People love to hate, they love to feel like part of a group, and they love to keep others out of the group. Immigrants, Jews, elites, zealots, do gooders, bookworms, commonists, scribes, you make them the problem, the enemies of the people, and you promise to let them have it.

31 And you have to play up patriotism, you have to make them think the most important thing in the world is Rome. The fatherland, that's what we're fighting for. To hell with anyone else, to hell with the colonies, and as for our enemies, they'd better watch out, or we'll crush them like bugs. Screw the rest of the world, you take what you can get and leave the losers to fight over the scraps. Rome First, that's what I always say.

32 You say, "I'll tell you what we're going to do, right? We get greedy, right? Now we're going to get greedy for Rome. We're going to grab and grab and grab. We're going to bring in so much money and so much everything. We're going to make Rome great again, folks, I'm telling you, folks, we're going to make Rome great again."

33 You have to know how to talk to these people, you have to know how to talk to the peasants. You have to tell them what they want to hear. Keep it simple, and repeat things, that's how you talk to them, because they're poorly educated. I love the poorly educated, they're easy marks.

34 The most important thing is, you have to know that politics, religion, business, it's all show biz. Put on a show, that's what you do. Jesus knew that, he never stopped putting on a show, and neither do I. At my rallies, I wear the very best togas, I put laurels in my hair, I get up on a dais, I stand tall, and I talk tough. You have to be like a gladiator, you have to look and talk and act like the baddest guy around.

35 I have a friend, he's from Hibernia, his name is MacMathuna. Hibernia, what a shithole country that is, it's worse than Britannia, and Britannia is

worse than Gaul. MacMathuna, he runs the gladiatorial games, like his father did before him. Only he's a genius at it, he's made it the biggest show in the Roman Empire. He's made billions, just like me.

36 He trains these gladiators to fight, of course you have to do that. But he also trains them how to put on a show—how to make an entrance, how to talk gruff, how to walk like a warrior, how to stick your chest out and stick your chin out and keep a look on your face like you're about to kill someone.

37 MacMathuna helped me plan my rallies, and boy was he good. He picked the music, he had his makeup people do my face and my hair, he had his costume designers dress me like a king. He set up the dais, he brought in shills to hype up the audience, he did it all.

38 He had me drive up in the biggest, baddest golden chariot in the empire, with the biggest black horses, and we left it sitting behind the dais the whole time. Horsepower, the people love it, that's what they want to see. If I had a flying machine, I'd come out of the clouds, like Jesus said he would, and I'd park it right there behind me. They'd eat that up, let me tell you.

39 People love that stuff, they eat it up at the games, and they eat it up in politics. A strongman, that's what they want. Everyone hates a bully, until they stand behind the bully and watch him kick the crap out of someone. If you don't believe me, you can ask my friends, the emperors. They know.

40 Julius Caesar, I didn't know him, but my grandfather saw him in Gaul, and my father, he was a warlord, he said Julius Caesar was the best general ever. They made him a god after he died, they made him the Divine Julius. He was something else, but he made one big mistake, I mean, really big. He let the Senate keep some power, and look what that got him—stabbed in the back by a bunch of senators, that's what.

41 Augustus, I didn't know him either, but he was smart, real smart. He was the son of a god, The Divine Son of the Divine Julius, and I mean, the *real* son of a *real* god, not like Little Jesus, the fake son of a fake god. Augustus *acted* like a god, he was worshipped in temples, he took power away from the Senate and the assemblies, he did it all his way.

42 When I got back to Rome after Jesus died, Tiberius Caesar was the emperor. Him I knew, I knew him well. My lawyer, my mentor Kohn, worked for him, and boy did they take care of business. If people crossed Tiberius or looked at him sideways, Kohn accused them of treason, tried them in court, executed them, and took everything they had. What a racket that was!

43 Kohn and Tiberius, they knew how to handle things, they were tough, tough as nails. If anyone attacks, you attack them back ten times harder. Attack, attack, attack. If anyone accuses you of something, you accuse them of something ten times worse. If anyone sues you, you sue them for ten times as much. And you never forget, and you sure as hell don't forgive, like that weakling Jesus said.

44 Kohn was a Jew, but back when I was young and first got to Rome, before I met Jesus and John the Batshit, this Kohn, he helped Tiberius kick all the Jews out of Rome. The Jews, they're troublemakers, they always make trouble for Rome. Kohn was smart, he knew who to be loyal to, and who to stab in the back.

45 Tiberius took all the power away from the senate, every last bit, he ran the show all by himself. I helped Tiberius, I did some work for him, me and Kohn were two of his top advisors. He killed anyone who got in his way, he even killed his own right-hand man. He even killed his own relatives to pave the way for my favorite emperor, Caligula.

46 My favorite emperor, that was Caligula, he was the best, he was my favorite. He could throw a party, let me tell you. He hired more of my dancing girls than anyone, and sometimes, when they went to his parties, they never came back. But what did I care, I was on the inside, and the times were good, they were real good.

47 Caligula did whatever he wanted, whenever he wanted. He used to say, when he was doing the worst of the worst, he'd say, "It's good to be king!" Sometimes, he went a little too far, but what can I say, it was always fun. Feasts, orgies, you name it, we did it.

48 He didn't just take power from the Senate, he killed any senator he didn't like. In fact, he killed anyone he felt like killing. He took any woman he wanted, and I don't mean he grabbed them by the delta—not that there's anything wrong with that—I mean he had his way with them, and then he bragged about it, sometimes right to their husbands. What could they do, he was the emperor!

49 In Egypt and Jerusalem, Caligula had himself worshipped as a god. In Rome, he dressed up like the gods and made the senators and everyone else worship him. What the hell, if you have absolute power, use it! I know I would. If you have power, but it's not absolute, do anything you can to make it absolute.

50 Eventually, Caligula killed so many people, and he took so many women, that some folks decided he had to go, and they assassinated him in a tunnel on the way to the theater. This theater, maybe it was one of mine, maybe it wasn't. I'm not going to say he deserved it, but yeah, maybe he deserved it.

51 After Caligula, Claudius was the emperor. I didn't think much of him, and he didn't let me in on his reign. So screw the bastard, who needs him. He did kick the Jews out of Rome, for the second time, after Tiberius. He let me keep my Jews, though, so what did I care.

52 Then comes Emperor Nero, Praise Be to Caesar! Nero Claudius Caesar Augustus Germanicus, now that's a name. Nero is my friend, I really like him, I'm his closest advisor. He's fun, not quite as fun as Caligula, but still fun. And he's tough, as tough as they come. Some people say he'd kill his own mother, in fact, the fake scribes say he did kill her. I don't know anything about that, I had nothing to do with it.

53 But back to the story, enough about emperors, back to Little Jesus. Nero, he'd been emperor for about six years when Peter and Paul came to Rome, spreading their scam and their crazy ideas right into the capital of the empire. The nerve of those two, at least Gabriel and Jesus were smart enough to hide out and stay as far away from Rome as they could.

54 Nero, he isn't a big fan of the Jews, he talks about them revolting sometime soon, how it's already started, and how he's going to crush them and throw down the Temple once and for all. And he's no fool. He knows a good

scapegoat when he sees one, and since Claudius threw the Jews out of Rome, he hasn't let them back in.

55 The Christians, most people consider them just a crazy bunch of Jews, sort of annoying, but nothing to get your toga in a wad over. Nero, he can't stand them, he thinks they're the worst of the Jews. But there aren't that many of them, so he'd hardly given them a second thought, at least not until that little fire last year.

56 So, to wrap up the story, a couple of years ago, I go to Nero, and I tell him, if we could get rid of some of the slums in the southern part of the city, we could build a development that would be better than the Forum. It would draw new business to Rome, and suck business out of the Forum, and it would be all ours, every inch of it, and every denarius that passed through, we'd get a cut.

57 And I tell him, while we're at it, why not let me, Donald of Gaul, renovate as many of the public buildings in Rome as I can? We could reshape the whole city in our image. And we could build him palaces the likes of which have never been seen.

58 Nero, he loved the idea. But how do we get rid of all those slums? If it was me, I'd just take it all, and use the law to do it. I tried that once, with that widow's house. I needed the land to park chariots for my casino, like I said, but back then, I didn't have enough stroke to get it done. Now I have all the stroke I need. But Nero, he waffled, he wasn't sure he wanted to go through with it.

59 Then, as luck would have it, a fire broke out, and I mean, it was big. It started near the Circus Maximus, and it spread like crazy. All those slums, they were full of crappy wooden houses, and they burned, and the wind, it carried the fire right up the Palatine Hill and across the Forum.

60 Lucky for me, my properties were all insured, I always insure them for more than they're worth. Overvalue for insurance, undervalue for taxes, that's how you do it. Kohen, my other Jew lawyer, he was a master at that, I have to give him credit.

61 That fire, it burned for a solid week, and it took out, like, two thirds of the city. People say there were gangs running around spreading the fire, and

chasing away anyone who tried to put it out. I don't know anything about that, I had nothing to do with it.

62 Thousands of people were killed, mostly in the slums. A lot of bums and beggars and poor people and homeless people, if they didn't die, they gave up and left the city. So some good did come out of the fire, in fact, a lot of good.

63 The whole city was thrown into chaos, and we got all kinds of things done because of it. No law, no rules, chaos is perfect if you want to throw your weight around, and Nero and me, we had all the weight, okay? If you want control, start by creating chaos, that's what you do, it works like a charm.

64 The best thing is that Nero and me, now we're building the Golden House, his palace, right where those disgusting slums used to be, and it's something to see. It's huge, really huge, three hundred rooms made of white marble, with mosaics on the floors, mosaics on the ceilings, frescoes on the walls, lots of theaters and bath houses, the works.

65 There's an eight-sided court, with a dome that rotates, and a hole in the roof to let in the sunlight, like the Pantheon. It's the greatest palace in the world, built by me, Donald of Gaul. On the outside, it's leafed with gold and inlaid with precious stones. There are hundreds of acres of gardens, and a manmade lake, and a statue of Nero over a hundred feet tall. You should see it, it's fantastic.

66 Inside, everything's covered with gold, right down to the toilets. Just like my palaces, I like everything covered with gold. My secretaries, they totally shower me with gold, you should see it, it's fabulous. Now Jesus, he can talk about heaven all he wants, and Gabriel, he can have his mansions, but this is the real deal, it's tremendous. My Golden House—make that, Nero's Golden House—will live forever.

67 Even more good came out of the fire than that. We've rebuilt a good portion of Rome, and she never looked better. And we've got more building, a lot more building, to do. Rome, built by me, Donald of Gaul. I should be able to put my name on everything I build, that's only fair, but no, Nero won't let me. But I know whose city this is, it's mine.

68 Best of all, Nero—I didn't have anything to do with it, don't believe what the fake scribes say—after the fire, Nero decided to get rid of the Christians once and for all by blaming the fire on *them*. The pagans hated the Christians already, they blamed bad things that happened on the Christians all the time. It's like I said, you need a good scapegoat sometimes.

69 So now, Nero rounds them up by the hundreds, and as long as they admit to being Christians, he kills them. You wouldn't believe how stubborn these people are, all they have to do is deny it, and he'll let them go. But no, they prefer to die for Jesus, their "Lord," they love him so much.

70 Nero, he's a creative guy. He plays the lyre, he writes music and stories, he acts and writes plays, he does all that crap. Now that he has thousands of Christians to kill, he does it with flair, like an artist.

71 He has huge parties that last all night long, and he hangs Christians up and burns them like torches for lighting. He has them crucified, mostly over by his palace, but some he hangs up all over the city, like decorations. And my favorite, he has them fed to dogs and bears and lions, and ripped limb from limb. That's a sight to see, it's terrific. We still kill a few now and then, just for kicks, like, when a party starts to fade.

72 But that's not all, it gets better! Peter and Paul, they've been in Rome causing trouble for about six years now. They're the leaders of the Christians, everyone knows it. Who better to make pay for the fire? So Nero, and I had nothing to do with it, Nero decided to execute them, too. Why not, the pagans would love it!

73 Aint Peter, they took him to the Golden House, and in the gardens there, at a place called Nero's Circus, where most of the Christians are executed, they crucified him. They didn't crucify him like they did Jesus, though—they turned the cross upside down instead, they crucified that loser standing on his head!

74 Jesus said that Peter was the "rock" that his church would be built on. Well, there's no church there, and there never will be, *that* I can tell you!

75 Paul the Apostate, they took him to a place south of the Golden House, and they tied him to a pillar. They couldn't crucify him, because he was a

Roman, so they beheaded him instead, just like Herod Antipasto beheaded John the Batshit.

76 The Christians, they say that when they chopped it off, Paul's head bounced three times, and where it hit the ground, three little springs shot up. Give these people credit, they have good imaginations, and they know how to make up a good story, but there aren't any springs there, believe me.

77 So now, Nero is the emperor, the Christians are on the run, the Jews in Judea are about to get crushed, Jesus and Gabriel haven't been seen for years, Peter and Paul are no more, and Donald of Gaul is the richest, most famous man in Rome. I've built the best buildings, I've advised the best emperors, I've had the best women.

78 But do I get any respect? No, these Romans, they still treat me like an outsider, and people say all kinds of bad things about me, and how many bad things I've done. Screw them, just look at the results. That's all that counts, what you have in the end, and I have more than *anyone* now, except Nero.

79 I wouldn't trade places with him, though, I hear he may be taking a long pisolino, a long nap, real soon! Don't ask me, I don't have anything to do with it, but that's what people are saying. And then, maybe I'll move into the Golden House myself.

80 As for Little Jesus, he's done. The Romans are out to get the Christians, and they'll wipe them out, Jesus and Gabriel included, as fast as you can say, "So long, sucker!" Not that I'll have anything to do with it, I won't, but within five years, there won't be any Christians left, anywhere in the empire. Now *there's* a prophecy for you, and I can guarantee it.

81 Sorry, Jesus! You lose! It's all over for you and your little scam.

82 Everyone loves a story with a happy ending. I'd like to end mine with a little quotation from Paul himself, that loser, something I hear he wrote to these two guys from Greece, these two Corinthians, that I had translated from Greek:

83 "If I make you sad, what will make me happy, if not the same thing that makes you sad?"

84 Amen to that, nothing feels better than giving the shaft to your enemies and screwing them, good and hard.

85 Vengeance is mine, Donald of Gaul's, and it sure is sweet. Amen.

AFTERWORD

No records concerning Donald of Gaul have been found, perhaps, some speculate, because they were destroyed in the Great Fire of Rome in 64 AD. Others speculate that Donald was erased from Roman history for collusion with the Pisonian Conspiracy to assassinate Emperor Nero in the following year. Both reasons may, of course, be true; regardless, it seems likely that he perished shortly after his gospel was completed in 65 AD.

How Donald died is up for debate. Hints in the text suggest that he was indeed a member of the Pisonian Conspiracy, several of whose co-conspirators were forced by Nero to commit suicide, including its leader, Gaius Calpernius Piso, the writer/philosopher Seneca, the poet Lucan, and the satirist Petronius.

Because Piso was a patron of literature, it has also been suggested that Donald's gospel may have been ghost written by someone in Piso's inner circle. A close analysis of the text supports this theory and suggests the authorship of Petronius, due in part to an undertone of satire that apparently went unnoticed by Donald.

According to the historian Tacitus, the Pisonian Conspiracy went deeper than was known at the time, as Piso was apparently marked for assassination immediately after taking power from Nero, to be replaced by Seneca. Such a plot would have made Seneca, not Marcus Aurelius, the first Philosopher King as imagined in Plato's *Republic*.

Several scholars who have studied Donald's gospel in detail believe that, at least for Donald, it wasn't Seneca, but Donald himself who was intended to be the ultimate beneficiary of the conspiracy.

Had Donald of Gaul successfully become the Emperor of Rome in 65 AD, he, not Nero, would likely have presided over the downfall of the Julio-Claudian dynasty, which ended instead with Nero's suicide in 68 AD. This dynasty oversaw the destruction of the Roman Republic and a rapid decline into increasingly decadent, depraved, and dictatorial rule under Caligula and Nero.

The Lost Gospel of Donald raises questions about the consequences for republicanism and public morality in the West if a person of such proclivities were to ascend to the peak of power today. Presumably, the strength of the West's political institutions, the power of her free press, the durability of her moral authority, and, above all, the decency of her Christian communities render such a scenario virtually impossible.